T0199163

The Book of
REVELATION

What It Says to Me

Robert Martin Schmidt

WESTBOW
PRESS®
A DIVISION OF THOMAS NELSON
& ZONDERVAN

Scripture taken from the King James Version of the Bible.

WestBow Press books may be ordered through booksellers or by contacting:

WestBow Press
A Division of Thomas Nelson & Zondervan
1663 Liberty Drive
Bloomington, IN 47403
www.westbowpress.com
1 (866) 928-1240

ISBN: 978-1-5127-2265-9 (sc)

Library of Congress Control Number: 2015920156

Print information available on the last page.

WestBow Press rev. date: 12/03/2015

Contents

Chapter One

The Bible has many books concerned with the story of Jesus's life, His birth, His testimony, and His resurrection. All these things have been done in the past, but one thing or group of things remains to do. Jesus has to come back to earth and delivers us to Himself. Jesus is also sending unbelievers to their judgment for not believing the power of the testimony of Jesus to redeem them from the world.

This book and the interpretation of its contents has blessing and a curse with it. The blessing is that God is given mankind early notice that the time for the end of mortal man is coming and the world needs to know these things to prepare for the coming events, has shown in the Book of Revelation of the things He is going to do and those things He will allow to happen to mankind during the tribulation. The Book of Revelation is for believers as well as unbelievers alike. Believers hope they will be delivered and the unbelievers hope that God will deliver them without becoming a believer. The curse that faces those who interpret Revelation by adding to its words or by subtracting from its words is not what a person should undertake unless he or she has been authorized by the Lord to do so.

Revelation 22: 18, 19 states, "For I testify unto every man who hears the words of this prophecy of this book. If any man shall add into these things God will shall add unto him the plagues that are written in the book and if any man take away from these words of the book of prophecy. "GOD SAYS HE SHALLTAKE AWAY HIS PART OUT OF THE BOOK OF LIFE (BLOTTED OUT) AND OUT OF THE HOLY CITY (CANNOT ENTER) AND FROM THE THINGS (BLESSINGS) WHICH ARE WRITTEN IN THIS BOOK". You can see that Revelation is different than other books of the bible. God wants to show mankind He means business (the end is near) and the Book of Revelation is the true authority of how the events of the last days will proceed. This is the only book in the bible that has eternal judgment in interpreting the book incorrectly and teaching others what it does not say or not say what does say. Even a Christian can lose his place in the afterlife if they teach or witness the contents in a false way (22: 18, 19) Revelation, even believers are not safe from judgment.

Chapter Two

As I discuss this book, I will not use many biblical verses to establish what I am trying to say; I will use what I believe is being said in the verses, but basically, I am establishing what I say like I was reasoning with myself and trying to establish an idea and a possible solution, while concentrating on the subject at hand. I will not use any books but the King James Version of the bible and a few other books in the bible, but (Revelation) will establish my reasoning for my answer. Remember, I am saying what (Revelation) says too me not what it says to others. It is up to you to decide what you accept or not accept. I did use a few verses in revelation to establish a point. I also used a verse or two from Ezekiel, Daniel, and Zechariah in the Old Testament about their prophecies, which are almost identical to the prophecies of Apostle John in Revelation.

There seems to be many things God has revealed over thousands of years to prep man for the final days. One thing about the Lord, He always provides plenty of warning; when He decides to enforce His plan for mankind.

Revelation was given to the Apostle John concerning what will be happening in the last days of mortal man on earth. Since he was the last apostle that was still alive, the rest of the other apostles had already given their lives for the testimony of Jesus. It seems fitting that John received the vision from God to write the last book of the bible. The Romans tried to kill him with boiling water, but had no effect on John, because God helped him through ordeal.

So John was put on a deserted island; thinking he would be shut off from the rest of the world and he would not be able to witness or teach the testimony of Jesus to the population anymore. We must remember that John described his vision of the future from his first century perspective.

They did not have planes, tanks, cars, rifles, and cannons or any other advanced technology during John's time period on earth. John had nothing in his history to help him describe accurately the visions before him. To be truthful, I do not think I could describe John's time very accurately. Of course, God knew that John could only describe the visions from that time period. When the last days do come; the people of the last days will be looking at the vision, as if in modern times.

What I am trying to say is that John's vision is so accurate in the twenty first century; it looks like a mirror image of what we people expect to happen, if things keep going as they are. I have noticed that John used the word (THEN) that seems to stop one vision and starts another vision. This will establish some kind of order in each vision. It keeps you from leaping around in all the visions and trying to give order to all that misery.

Chapter Three

Revelation starts with the Lord Jesus standing in the midst of seven candlesticks; which are the seven churches of Asia. The Lord begins to warn the leaders of each church of John and tells them they need to correct some things to be right with God. They have little time to correct their disobedience and repenting. Each church except two was in need of repentance and correct the works needed to be done to get the approval of God. The Lord was not in any way impressed with the church. If things that needed to be corrected were not corrected; it could be punished by being blotted out of the Book.

There are rewards for those churches who listened to the Lord and corrected their problems that the Lord pointed out to them. The opposite of rewards is judgment; so if you do not do what you supposed to do you will be judged. The rewards are for those who obey the Lord.

The Lord did not beat around the bush on what was wrong with five of the seven churches of Asia; two of the churches were without fault; the five others were told what was wrong and how to fix it. Those deep in sin would probably not do as the Lord commanded, but repentance would be an option if they changed their mind.

The first thing noticeable in John's vision of the seven churches of Asia was they were independent from each other, yet part of a larger body as a whole. If you reason this out, it would show that each individual church would get their individual reward are be punished, according to their works.

It does not say in Revelation that salvation is the only gift of God; we have God, Jesus, Holy Spirit, New Earth, Holy City and Eternal Life. There are other rewards also.

The seven churches and how they can get the approval of God:

Ephesus------needs to get back to the first works, make Lord first in their lives; if they repent. And do those things commanded by God. The (reward) will be the right to eat from the Tree of Life.

Smyrna------be faithful until death; when Satan puts you in prison to be tried. Your (reward) will be the crown of life and the Second Death will have no power (Only the 144,000 resurrected Jews were given this power at the First Resurrection).

Pergamos-------some in your church hold the doctrine of Balaam; which has put a stumbling block before the children of Israel to eat forbidden foods and commit adultery before the Lord. You also hold the doctrine of the Nicolaitans; which the Lord hates. The Lord tells them to repent or He will come with a sword to correct the problem. If corrected, the (reward) will be able to eat the Holy Manna and you will be given a white stone with a new name on it and only you and the Lord know what that name is.

Thyatira------allowed the woman Jezebel to teach my servants to commit fornication and eat the forbidden food. Time to repent, but if not; I will kill her children and put great tribulation on those who does these things. He that sins will be the one punished; if they repent they will be spared. Their (reward) will be power over the nations and be given the brightness of the morning star; if they hold fast until the Lord returns.

Sardis------your works are dead; strengthen what is left and do not let it die. (Repent) not all of you are guilty and will walk with me in white clothing. (Reward) He that overcomes will not be blotted out of the Book of Life and I Jesus will confess him before the Father.

Philadelphia------Works are known, you have an open door, and you have kept my name and my word. I will keep you from the hour of temptation and/or wrath; that will come to all on the earth. Hold fast to crown,(Reward) be given the name of God, the name of the Holy City of Jerusalem and Jesus will write your new name on you and this will be your eternal name.

Laodicea------works are not cold or hot; you are lukewarm; and there is no middle ground to stand on.

You say in your heart you are rich and need nothing. God says, you are poor, miserable and blind and naked also. You need to anoint your eyes; so you can see the truth. (Repent) and overcome, and your (Reward) will be, sit on throne with Jesus just like God let Him sit down on His throne.

After you read about the seven churches of Asia. You will come to a conclusion that each church is different than the other churches. You will also notice each church has different problems than the other six. Of course, there is sin in every church, but in this case God is highlighting what is wrong with the churches Him Each will get different rewards for repenting and obeying the Lord; if they repent not and do not change their hearts back to the things of God; they will be cut off and their name removed from the Book of Life.

It is obvious to those who read about the seven churches, that there are different problems confronting each church and different rewards to those who repent and do as the Lord asks.

It may be that shadows all and that punishment is number one (Being blotted out of the Book of Life is about as bad as it gets).

Chapter Four

There are more questions than answers; when it comes to figuring out the deeper things concerning the seven churches of Asia. (Staying in Revelation) One of these questions; is how a believer be blotted out of the Book of Life? It shows that once saved; always saved is not a true interpretation. It shows that a believer could be blotted out of the Book of Life in many places in the New and Old Testament. What bothers me the most about being erased from the Book; is it goes against everything I have been taught over the years? After looking back at my biblical life. I noticed that many verses are direct and not up to interpretation; yet man has ignored and passed by to form a different solution or answer to fit their doctrine. Regardless of what people. Come up with to fix their doctrines, there are some things, which need to be straighten out before the Lord shows up. (There are black and white verses in the Bible and Revelation too). It is best that we use the dark verses, as well as, the feel good verses to establish a more docile or direct witness for the Lord.

I think that some believers have come to the point in their lives, that truth is not worth the suffering or persecution (I am no exception). Everyone wants the easy road to heaven and the easy way out of their problems, they (me) will try to take the easy way if the opportunity arises, every time, because we are just flesh in our nature.

Since a believer can be blotted out of the Book of Life; according to what has been implied in the first few pages of this book. What is a believer during the time of John and the writing of Revelation? In this case, the God of the Bible is the only belief system (compare bible with bible). So a believer would be a Christian, because he has to be or should be in the Book of Life. You cannot be a believer if you are not in the Book of Life. It is possible for a believer to be in the Book of Life and not be a believer yet, because their time has not yet come on them. It is logical that a person can be in the Book of Life and die without becoming a believer (baby etc.) The Book of Life is absolute in deciding who goes where on Judgment Day (believers and unbelievers).

Chapter Five

We need to get back to a study of the rewards and judgments of the seven churches of Asia. The Lord always closes each statement about the seven churches of Asia with another statement; "He that has an ear, let him hear what the spirit says to the churches". Notice He says churches not church. As far as I can tell, the Lord did not say to all the churches, He would "keep them from the hour of temptation," but singled out, Philadelphia alone. You can take this premise of reasoning to any of the other churches with the same results.

Of course, we believers in the last days can assume each of the seven churches of Asia will get the same rewards, including the reward to deliver the church from the hour of temptation (Wrath to come) in the last days. As much as I want to believe that we can escape the wrath to come; I cannot in any way in Revelation find the verses or spiritual justification, to say, that we are going to be out of here before the Tribulation starts or be dead; which is another way to escape the wrath to come and go to heaven. You just die without facing long term suffering. One question I have about all Seven Churches of Asia in the last days. Are they going to be judged together or as one unified seven member church or they going to be judged separately?

I know that I spent a lot of time on the church of Philadelphia. It does seem that the Philadelphia and Smyrna church is the shining example of what God expects of His church and a good representative to the other churches.

The Lord also said about the Philadelphia church, that they had an open door to the throne of God, and no man can close it. You have little strength, but you have not denied my name. Hold fast to what you have and do not let no man take your crown. He that over comes I will make him a pillar in the temple of my God and he will have no need to go outside the temple again and I will also make those of the assembly of Satan, which say they are Jews, to come and worship you on their knees and know in their hearts that God loves you very much. The Lord also said about the church of Smyrna, another good example of a church that God approved. God says, I know your works, and your tribulation, and your poverty, but you are rich before God. Do not fear those things that you are about to suffer. Notice how the Philadelphia church does not want to suffer the tribulation and the Smyrna church has been chosen to suffer the tribulation. Lord says, some of you will be cast into prison, to be tried, you shall have tribulation for ten days and be faithful until death, and I will give you a crown of life.

You have probably noticed, that the church of Philadelphia will avoid the hour of wrath or temptation; according to verse in Revelation which does not mean that you are going to be taken up into the clouds to avoid any hardships that are going to face all on the earth during the last days. You will simply will be moved out of the way.

What I think will happen? The Lord will have some place to hid the Philadelphia church or be taken up to Jesus on a cloud, like some people believe today. Strange that one church gets delivered and another has to face up to the tribulation period. All will suffer the tribulation events (good people and evil people).

John says after these visions of the churches ended; he was caught up in the spirit and the first thing he saw was a throne being set up in heaven and He that sat on the throne had the appearance of jasper and sardine stone around the throne like an emerald. John saw twenty four elders clothed in white sitting around the throne and each had a gold crown on their heads, and as he looked at the throne, there came lightings, thunders and voices. There were seven lamps burning before the throne (Seven spirits of God) and a sea of glass stretched out before the throne, it appeared like a form of crystal.

There were four beasts around the throne (same beasts of Ezekiel's prophecy), each was full of eyes all around them (front, back, sides). First beast was like a lion, the second like a calf, the third had a face of a man, and the fourth beast was like an eagle in flight with wings outset. Each beast had six wings and many eyes within their wings. These beasts' never rested day or night.

There were many people that were standing before the throne and many angels praising God and all praise was directed to the throne.

Chapter Six

Where God sits, it gave God great pleasure in creating all that was created. Man also creates things that he takes pride or pleasure in, but if it does not turn the way it is expected too. It will be redone, reshaped, or destroyed. The creator will try to figure out what went wrong and correct the problem. Mankind has not lived up to their calling also, by causing sin and rebellion toward God and His laws. So like us humans, the problem needs to be corrected and the time and events will eventually end sin and rebellion on earth. This is the reason why the Lord had the Book of Revelation written. It was to show and warn every man and women that God is serious about cleaning up His creation and bring peace and order to the earth. There is no middle ground and there is no one but you that can make that decision for you.

Chapter Seven

We need to go back to the four beasts we discussed earlier and talk about those that have been created to have free choice and those who were created to not have choice. We must remember that when we believers get to heaven and we have an opportunity to go before the throne of God. We will see the four beasts we discussed earlier in Revelation in constant praise toward God and His greatness. These beasts were created for the sole purpose of giving God endless praise. They have no freewill nor the need of freewill. Mankind was created to be in constant praise and worship of God, but the praise and worship given to God is by free choice/ freewill. Mankind freely gives praise and worship out of love for the Lord Jesus and what he has done on the Cross.

Revelation and other books of the bible that show the events of the last days are confusing, because of the weird looking beasts and animals, used to explain the final days and the hardships that mankind will face at that time. These hardships on man will help cause non-believers of the testimony of the Lord Jesus to become believers. Even if you have free choice, but you have only two choices: Heaven or the Lake of Fire, there is no middle ground and there is no one, but you that can make that decision We have been created to have free choice and those who were not created to have free choice. We must remember that when we believers get to heaven and we have an opportunity to go before the throne of God. We will see the four beasts we discussed earlier in constant praise toward God and his greatness. These beasts were created for the sole purpose the giving endless praise to God. They have no freewill nor the need for freewill. Mankind was created to be in constant praise and worship of God, but the praise and worship given to God is by free choice/ freewill. Mankind freely gives praise and worship out of love for the Lord Jesus and what He has done on the Cross.

God the father is spirit and totally invisible to mankind and the heavenly host of characters, but God the Father can speak out of things that make Him seem visible to those who have vision in heaven and earth. No one has ever seen God at any time, except Jesus; He sees God because He is God with a human form. Jesus is the total sum of the God of all creation. Jesus is the flesh God we see and Jesus is the spirit God we do not see. In the history of Israel and the bible; we have had characters in the bible who thought they saw God in one form or another, but God the father will always be Spirit and He will always come in has His own body and has no need of another body. He has the same kind of body we will get when we are resurrected in the last days

Chapter Eight

Getting back to Revelation. We see John looking around at the great sight of the Throne of God; when suddenly the right hand of God produced a book with seven seals and one of the angels proclaimed in a loud voice to all that was present, "Who is worthy to open the book and break the seals? "There were no one in heaven or earth found worthy of such a great honor. This bothered John; when no one could be found that he started to cry. One of the twenty-four elders came over to him and told him to quit crying, because there was one man worthy and he would be represented by a slain lamb, with seven eyes and seven horns; these are things that represent the seven spirits of God that are on the whole earth. Jesus walked up to the throne and took the book out of God's hand, because he was the only one found worthy to take the book and break its seals. Jesus was worthy before God, because He poured out His life on the cross in obedience to God's will and not His own will. When Jesus took the book, everyone in heaven and earth fell down to worship Him as God. There were millions and millions of angels around the throne giving praise to God and His Son. (Jesus opened the first seal), one of the four beasts around the throne told John to come and see what was about to happen. There came a notice like thunder when the seal was opened. He was given a crown and sent to earth to conquer or make war. John saw a white horse and a person sitting on it; but he had a bow with no arrows

(Then) the second seal was opened and John was asked by the second beast around the throne to look at a red horse that was leaving to destroy all peace on the earth.

(Then) the third seal was opened and the third beast of the throne wanted John to come and see what is happening. Out came a black horse with a pair of balances in his hand. He was to bring balance/equality on the foodstuff of the world like wheat and barley. Food will be scarce at this time, but you will be able to buy a measure of wheat for a penny or you could get a lesser grade of food like barley in three measures for a penny. The oil and wine is to be left alone for now. There seems to be something more to add to the black horse vision. I think at this time the black horse and his mission is to project two kinds of people, after all the wars are over. There will be a shortage of food and other things. These things will be at a price and the best food, wine, and oil will be given to those who can pay for it and the poor will have to survive on the lower grade foodstuffs.

(Then) the fourth seal was opened and the fourth beast of the throne asked John to come with him to see what was about to happen. Out came a pale horse with death and hell as its rider. Power was given to them to destroy twenty-five percent of the population of the earth by the sword, hunger, and with death by animals and the beasts of the field. Twenty-five percent of probably seven billion people on earth at this time; this would be about 1.8 billion being killed at this time, leaving about 5.2 billion still alive.

Then the fifth seal was opened and an altar was visible with the many souls that were slain for their testimony of the Lord Jesus. They were crying out to God to avenge their deaths on earth; each of them were given white robes and told to rest a little longer, until their fellow servants were killed like they were killed for their testimony of Jesus. (Then) the sixth seal was opened and it released a great earthquake that filled the sky with ash, this caused the sky to become blacken and the light of the moon to become blood red and ash made the light on earth to become dull.

The stars of the heavens begin to fall to the earth like a fig tree dropping its fruit in an unorderly or untimely way. In a high wind one may fall here and another one over there. There is no orderly fashion how or where the fruit will fall. After that all, of the heavens are rolled up like a scroll. This means that the scroll will be rolled up from the outside to the inside to the throne itself; so in a way the universe is going to collapse on itself and go back to its beginning.

If you reason out this event it will make perfect sense to you. (First) Did not God say He was going to create a new heaven and a new earth? You have to remove the old heaven before you can replace with a new heaven. (Second) Did not God say? He was going to create a new earth to replace the one Satan corrupted and replace it with a new one for His people and the new throne of God, which will be in Jerusalem. God the father and the Lord Jesus will rule from there forever with His people. This event will cause great mountains to move out of their place, even islands will suffer and be no more. These events will be happening through the earth and the universe.

They will plead with the mountains to fall on them; to hide them from the face of the Lamb and His wrath on the people of the earth.

The Day of His Wrath has finally come, as Jesus said it would happen upon the earth. No one can say they were not warned of this day from the scriptures. Who will be able to stand before Jesus? No one will be standing, all will be on their faces begging Jesus to be merciful. After all these things happened, I John saw four angels standing on the four corners of the earth. One angel facing each direction: (North, South, East, West). They were to hold the four winds of the earth at bay. There will no longer any wind on the earth: none on the sea, none on the trees. The earth will become quite and silent.

John sees an angel coming from the east with a seal of God in his hands. Begins telling the four angels to not hurt anything on earth, until all believers are sealed in their foreheads with the seal of God. There were 144,000 total from the tribes of Israel. Each tribe was represented by 12,000 of its members. There were 12 tribes in the house of Israel. (12,000 x 12= 144,000)

John says after this had happened, there appeared a great multitude of people before the throne that could not be numbered from all the nations of the world.

Each was wearing white clothing and holding a palm branches in their hands. Everyone was shouting to the Lord "Salvation to our God, and the lamb (Jesus) who sits on the throne." Everybody including the angels of God fell on their faces and worshipped God and His Son; Giving God His due for being such a merciful God. All the people worshipping God in white robes were those who came out of the great tribulation and had their robes washed in the blood of Jesus.

The above biblical verses poses a problem for some doctrines that are being preached in the twenty-first century; especially the going up doctrine into the clouds before the tribulation doctrine. There was nothing said about the departure of the believers from the earth before the tribulation, but only those who came out of the Great Tribulation. As I see it, there are angels and people with white robes present after the Great Tribulation at the throne of God; these people are the only ones present at this time. Besides, look at this doctrine from a different view; as I said before, John sees only angels and people coming out of the Great Tribulation. Where are the saints of older days? Where are those people who hold to the pre- tribulation doctrine of going to meet Jesus in the air? Why did God put great blessings on those who came out of the Great Tribulation and not mention the rest of the believers? Seems to me, all believers (angels and people) were present at this worshipping of God service, no one was excluded or given special treatment not to be there. So this would say to me, that the only ones not there were Satan and his fallen angels and all unbelievers of the testimony of Jesus.

Chapter Nine

The seventh seal was opened and a terrible silence fell on heaven for about 30 minutes. Seven angels were given seven trumpets. Another angel was given a golden censer with a lot of incense to mix with the prayers of the saints on the golden altar of God that was before the throne of God. The smoke of incense and prayers ascended up to God. The angel took the censer and filled it with fire from the altar and cast it down to earth. There begin to be all sorts of things start to happen: voices, thunder, lighting, and large earthquakes. After all these things took place, the seven angels who had the seven trumpets were getting ready to blow their individual trumpets in the order God had chosen. For each trumpet brought a different woe of wrath to the earth and its people.

The first angel blew his trumpet and hail and fire mixed with blood were cast down on the people of the earth causing 33% of the trees to be burned up and all the grass.

The second angel blew his trumpet and a great mountain burning with fire landed in the sea and 33% of the sea became blood or blood-like. 33% of the sea creatures of things living in the sea died and 33% of all ships were destroyed. I believe that only a big rock (asteroid) from space hitting in the sea could cause such an event to happen. There is no power on earth, including nuclear, that can damage or destroy 33% of our world in one event.

The third angel blew his trumpet and a great star from heaven came down on the rivers and 33% of all freshwater was made bitter. Seems to me that John was seeing the after effect of a nuclear entry and explosion; which leaves water bitter because of the radiation it gives off. Regardless of what we think these falling stars to be; it had a great effect on the fresh water supply on earth and many men and women died from not having fresh water to drink. I personally think these stars from heaven were nuclear missiles entering into our atmosphere. They would probably look like falling stars if you saw the flame of the engines burning as they came down.

After this, the fourth angel blew his trumpet. 33% of the light on earth, sun, moon, and stars was reduced because of the presence of ash clouds that were in our atmosphere from nuclear explosions and volcano activity. The more ash and dust in the atmosphere the more dimmer the light we see on earth. The above statement does not mean that the sun, moon, and stars are going to be cut up in thirds, it just means the light from these objects will be dimmer because of the ash and dust in our atmosphere. After this had taken place, John saw an angel flying across the sky telling everyone on earth to prepare for the last three trumpet angels to blow their trumpets and woe to them on earth:

Then the fifth angel blew his trumpet once and a great star (angel) fell from heaven to earth with a key to open the bottomless pit. He opened the bottomless pit and much smoke came out, and the air was darken because of the smoke and out of the smoke came locusts on the earth. The locusts had the same power as a scorpion. They could sting mankind with their tails. But they had no power to hurt grass, or any green thing. Their mission was to torment those men and women who did not the seal of God on their foreheads for five months. Being tormented in this fashion would cause many to seek death, but the power to die would be kept from them. They would be tormented by the locusts until the time given by God to stop the torment.

Locusts pictured by John is a locust of this time period, but somewhat like a horse being dressed for a coming battle. On their head was something like a crown of gold and their faces appeared as human faces. They had long hair and teeth like a lion. They also had wings and when they took off; they sounded like many chariots moving in the background. Their tails were like the tail of a scorpion, with the power to sting mankind for five months. There was the presence of leadership, who was the king of the bottomless pit (Satan). The first woe has passed. (This locust could be a modern tank, and planes fly; they were some special locust with the power to inflect pain.) Also you must remember they came out of the same bottomless pit Satan had been confined too.

The second woe and third woe is coming next. Remember the angel flying across the sky, saying: Woe, Woe, Woe, three times to the inhabitants of the earth.

Then the sixth angel blew his trumpet and John heard a voice coming out of the four beasts of the golden altar of God saying to the 6th angel, Loose the four angels that are bound to the Euphrates river. They were set free to kill 33% of the remaining population of the earth. They were prepared by God for this purpose and moment in time. There were over 200,000,000 oriental troops coming from the East to kill 33% of the remaining human population in that area of the world. The Euphrates River needs to dry up to allow the army from the East to crossover into the Middle East. When the time is right the river will dry up.

The Oriental Army and their people had little to do with the earth's problems until the 20th century. If you read the bible closely you will see very little mention of the oriental people until the time of the last days; then all of a sudden, they become a major player in the events of the world. It seems like the destiny of the oriental population was always before us, but not for us. God kept them in the background for end time use.

Back to John's vision, John saw in a vision the horsemen and their horses. They had breastplates of fire, brimstone, and Jacinth. We that live in the 21th century know the oriental people have a flare with bright colors, designs, and their tradition. Horses were dressed up to scare their enemies of their viciousness. John said the horse's heads looked like a lion; but they were purposed to kill 33% of mankind, by smoke, fire, and brimstone. All the weapons of the 21st century are capable of carrying out the vision of John and the types of death that will be put on mankind. Remember everyone that the main players in the last days are: Israel, Russia, China, European Union, Middle East (United States will not be a major player in the last days). Will probably fall by the sword, or civil unrest, or the (Economy), which will be main event early in the tribulation or maybe the United States falls apart from over extension of their forces in the world.) U.S. does not exist at all in scripture. Unless it is the Babylon of Revelation

After that vision had passed. John saw a mighty angel come down from heaven surrounded by a cloud and had a rainbow on his head. His face was like bright sunlight and his feet was like fire. You would probably think this angel was Jesus because of the rainbow on his head and He fits the other descriptions in the Bible. Remember in the kingdom of God. The residents may not look as we look, they might look differently, but we are all equal in Jesus. The body of Jesus is and always will be the only perfect body of God and be occupied by God Himself and His Son and the Holy Spirit.

The angel put his right foot in the sea and his left foot on the land. Which probably says to us that whatever that was going to happen will fall on the sea and on the land. The angel had a little book that was opened in his hands. He cried out in a loud voice like a lion roaring and out of the book came seven thunders. John started to write what the seven thunders had said, but a voice from heaven told John not to let it be known what the seven thunders had said until the latter days, then at the appointed time, the contents will be revealed. After this the angel raised his hand to heaven and gave worship and great praise to God and made the statement that time will be no more. There will be no need for time or measured motion anymore. Everything has been made eternal.

Chapter Ten

When the seventh angel sounds his trumpet. The mystery of God will be finished just as He was stated in the scriptures. John was told from heaven to eat the little book; so John went up to the angel who had the little book. The angel told him to eat the little book, but informed John that the book will taste like honey but be bitter in your stomach.

The little book in the angels' hands contained the seven thunders; which showed John that something was about to happen that was pleasing and sweet to man, but afterwards it left a bitter taste and not as pleasing as first thought.

The angel told John he was to witness before many nations and tongues. The book of Revelation that was written about the end days is a great witness to the people that are loyal to their faith in Jesus with great hope and a great desire to be with him. Revelation is also a book that condemns mankind and still warns the people that time is running out and the time to repent is now. Remember your last breath is your final decision to repent or not. Your decision to repent or not repent dies with your last breath, you are off the clock and no longer have a place in the world of the living if your decision was negative. The reason I think the little book contained the seven thunders is because the seventh and final trumpet blast has been sounded. And in the book of Daniel these prophecies were to be reveled in the latter days and I do not think you can get no more latter days than they are now. So I can see that the seven thunders are soon to make themselves known in these end times.

Chapter Eleven

One vision ends and another one begins for John. John was given a rod to measure the Temple of. God, the Altar, and the people who worship there. John was not to measure the court, because it belonged to the Gentiles and they were going to thread the courts for 42 months. Two men will be given power from God, dresses in sackcloth (very low grade garment) to be a witness and preach the word of God for 42 months. These two people are special witnesses for the Lord; No one will be allowed to harm them and if some try harm the two witnesses, the witnesses can kill them by speaking the word. These two witnesses have the power to stop all rain on the earth. They have the power to turn water into blood and to smite the earth with any curse or plaque they choose.

After the two witnesses have completed their testimony; the beast that is in the bottomless will make war with the two witnesses and kill them. He will let their bodies go unburied for three and one half days. The people will be very happy that the people who cause all these misery on them are finally dead. They will have parties and give gifts in celebration, but after three and one-half days the two witnesses will come back to life and rise from the earth to heaven on a cloud. The enemies of the two witnesses were speechless. Since I have not ever seen such a sight before. I think this vision would cause me to rethink my position.

In the same hour that the witnesses were going up to heaven, there came a great earthquake and 10% of Jerusalem fell and seven thousand men were killed and those who remained were terrified about what had happened and finally gave God the glory. The third woe came quickly after the above events. And the seventh trumpet sounded with a great blast. All kingdoms of the world now belong to the Lord Jesus and GOD, and Jesus will reign forever and all the nations of the world will gave great praise to GOD and His Christ.

After this event, there was a wonder in heaven, a women clothed in the sun's brightness and had the light of the moon under her feet. She had a crown of twelve stars. She was with child (Israel) and begin to show signs of labor and about to deliver. Right after this another wonder appeared in heaven; a great red dragon with seven heads and ten horns and seven crowns on his head. The dragon was standing there to waiting for the man child to be delivered.

This dragon (Satan) had one third of heavens angels to do his bidding and they were cast out of heaven to the earth. The dragon was waiting for the child to be born so it could kill it or eat it. She gave birth to Jesus but was quickly taken to heaven by God to the throne of God. God had already prepared a place for the woman (Israel) to hide from the dragon after the Child was born. There they would hidden and fed for three and one half years.

At this time a great war in heaven is being fought. God's angels were fighting Satan's angels; but God's angels prevailed and cast Satan and his angels out of heaven to the earth. After this had been done. A loud voice proclaimed that the constant accuser of the brethren of God was no longer able to accuse the brethren, day or night, before the throne of God. Satan was permanently removed from heaven and could not no more make complaints about the people of God on earth.

The people of God overcame Satan and his angels by the blood of Jesus, the Lamb of God and their testimony of Him. They were willing to give their lives to follow Jesus to their deaths Happy are those in heaven at this time, but Woe to them on earth, because Satin and his entire army of demon followers were cast earth. Satan knows he has but a short time to accomplish his goals. Once he realized he was on earth. He began to hunt down the people of God, because they had conceived the Man-child (Jesus). The woman (Israel) was given the ability to get into the wilderness for safety and Israel will be fed and watered there foe three and one-half years and will be hid from the dragon. Satan tried to kill the woman with a flood of water aimed at her, but God had the earth opened up and swallowed the water. Satan decided to hunt down what was left alive of the remaining seed which followed the Lord and his testimony.

Chapter Twelve

John says he was placed on the seashore were he saw a great beast rise up out of the sea (people). It had seven heads and ten horns with crowns on each head of the beast with blasphemy written on each head. John said the beast was similar to a leopard with feet of deer, a mouth of a lion, and Satan gave him great power and authority. The great beast had what appeared to be a wound in its head and he appeared to be dead and yet he came back to life. The people of the world marveled at this great miracle and chose to be loyal to him, because he had the ability to heal himself. The beast was given a mouth piece (a person) to speak for him to those people of the world who were loyal to him at this time. The beast only had 42 months to exist. So he was not holding back on curses to God and God's Throne, and everyone who dwelled in Heaven.

It was given to the beast the power to make war with the saints (believers) and defeat them. He was then given power to rule over the whole earth (one world government.) Everyone name that is not written in the book of life will worship the Beast. God says, if you can hear you best listen: He that leads people into captivity will go into captivity themselves, He that kills people will be killed themselves. So we believers will be required to hold on to our faith and maintain our patience in enduring these things. Remember only the flesh dies, heaven awaits the believers and the lake of fire awaits the unbelieving. Remember also, you can repent up to the time you die; once death happens (Decision time is over).

Chapter Thirteen

Then John says he saw another beast come out on the earth. It had two horns like a lamb, but had the voice of a Dragon and he had the same power of the first beast. He caused everyone to worship the first beast because he had been dead, but came back alive with his own power. He could make fire come down from heaven (Not God's Heaven) just the sky above the earth. These miracles that are being done by the beast are deceiving those who dwell one earth; he only has these powers when the first beast is present. The second beast wanted to make an image (statue) to the first beast; so the first beast could have the power to speak for himself, because he was wounded by the sword and yet lived. The second beast had power to give life to the statue of the first beast and all that did not worship the statue of the first beast would be killed. The second beast caused all people of the earth to receive a mark on their right hand, or on their forehead. Remember the Mark of the Beast will be on your right hand, not your left hand. On your forehead or in your forehead, In your forehead is to me, is not a stamp on your forehead, or device put in your head, but something like brain activity (like a pin number) you can remember for yourself. I do not know what the motive would be for getting such an invisible number in place of the other options; maybe its vanity or someone thinks they can hide the mark from God on the day of His reckoning. God made known these places for the mark of the beast available to you through His word, you have no excuse not knowing about the mark's position on your body.

No one could buy or sell without the mark; this means you cannot buy food or anything. You or at the mercy of the people who have the mark to buy food and things for you who do not have the mark. I personally think those who except food and things from the mark holders are in a way, saying, Satan is providing our needs, not God. And I am absolutely sure that Satan and his cronies will use this situation to fool some of the people who are not been marked to get marked, because of the great need for food, clothes, etc. I think this situation concerning the mark of the beast is the most horrible event that can happened to the people of the earth. Remember the world is coming out of great wars and there are not much food or anything else left on the planet to use to keep mankind alive. Times will be hard for mankind, and as I said before, Satan will use this circumstance to show the people he is able to provide what they need, not God. Also there is something else to think about; without food, or water, you are going to die anyway, if you were injured because of world turmoil's, such as injuries, lack of water, no food, disease of all kinds, the probabilities' are you will die anyway if you take the mark of the beast. Why take a chance of losing heaven for a few days of food, water etc. My advice to you and me also, do not take any Mark of any kind on your body or any accept any mark mentality.

The number of the beast is 666, and I do not know who or what it is. I think the mark of the beast has a lot more to do with information about the person themselves. The people are freely giving everything about themselves to Satan by accepting the mark. (Remember) Satan is not all knowing. He only knows what you tell him or show him; getting the mark would leave Satan knowing all about you.

I have a few ideas of what the mark of the beast could be: 1) the mark could be an unnoticeable computer chip, everybody knows how small they make them in today's world. 2) IT could be a tattoo of some kind which could; easily be put on your right hand or forehead and be visible to others. 3) It could be an access number or some kind of pin number that gives Satan the ability to know everything about you. BASICALLY THE MARK OF THE BEAST IS NOTHING BUT A MARK SHOWING THE BEAST FULL OWNERSHIP OF THE PERSON RECEIVING THE MARK.

Chapter Fourteen

As John was looking around, he saw Jesus the Lamb of God standing on Mt. Zion and He had 144,000 Jews with him, having God's name written (on) their foreheads. Then John says he heard a voice from heaven like many waters (people praising God at one time) as the voice of great thunder; plus there were many harps playing in the background. The 144,000 Jews were singing a new song before God and those around the throne. This song could not be sung by anyone but the 144,000 Jews that were resurrected in the first resurrection. These Jews were without fault before God and were not defiled by women and wherever the Lord went they would follow.

The 144,000 Jews were the first fruits of the first resurrection; they are the Jews that were beheaded for the cause of Christ (This is totally biblical) the beheaded 144,000 Jews are the First Resurrection. No one in mass numbers was ever resurrected before this time and even then; they appeared only for a short time to prove a point for God and then back to heaven they went. Besides Jesus was resurrected one time from death. The 144,000 Jews will not be resurrected again; nor will they need too. The believer dies once and is resurrected once, the (unbeliever is resurrected once and dies twice). This means you die in the flesh once and later the body is cast into Lake of Fire which is the second death. The body of the believers must die before it can be resurrected, even if you are alive at the Resurrection, your body will have to die before you get your new body; but it is done in the twinkle of the eye. So you may not realize it has happened. Just think about having a new body; one that has no pain or need for anything the old body required to survive in the mortal world.

Chapter Fifteen

The Church is not the first fruits of the first resurrection; it is not the time for them to be resurrected from the earth. It was appointed by God Himself for the works of the Jewish believers; but not all of them. And yes, there are more than the 144,000 believing Jews that will be resurrected with the rest of the believing gentiles on the Last Day. We believers must face the fact we are not needed to participate in the world affairs and events after the seven years of tribulation has passed and the 1000 year reign begins. The 144,000 Jews of the First resurrection will be not be removed from the earth. They will be judges and priests during the 1000 year reign of Jesus on earth. There will be many believers in heaven after The Great Tribulation, a number so great no one can count.

There has always been a problem in theology over when the Gentile believers will be resurrected and when the non-believers will resurrected. There are many believers who think the Church will be resurrected before the tribulation begins. This is possible but not likely, God never changes; if you die before the tribulation and you are a believer you will be in heaven; if you die during the tribulation and you are a believer you will be in heaven; if you die during the end of the Great Tribulation and are a believer you will go to heaven. Basically everyone who dies and are believers will be raptured or be transported to heaven. But the Bible does say the Second Resurrection will be great event. This is why I think the Final Resurrection will be after the 1000 year reign, so God will end all things that were, to those things that will be.

The non-believers are transported to Hell after death. Those people who died without accepting the testimony of the Lord. But like everyone else, believers and unbelievers, when you die you are transported to your holding area. Believers go to Paradise and non-believers go to Hell, until the Great White Throne Judgment is finished with its work. I have always wondered who will live in the 1000 year reign of the Lord. I think that I am close to an answer. There will probably be seven billion people on the earth when the tribulation period begins. 25% of the world's population will be killed during the first few years of the tribulation; which will be about 1.75 billion out of seven billion killed, leaving 5.25 billion on earth still alive.

- Toward the end of the Great Tribulation. There will be 30% of the remaining people on earth that will be killed. 30% of these 5.25 billion that were left from the first part of the tribulation is 157.5 billion leaving 3.5 billion people on earth.

- These 3.5 billion people left will be the ones that will go to the 1000 year reign of Christ.
- There will not be any saved people on earth during the 1000 year reign. Except Jesus and the 144,000 Jews. They will be Kings and Priests of the people of the 1000 year reign.
- The sole reason for the 1000 year reign is to provide a chance for them to accept the Lord without Satan there to influence them.
- Remember God is in the business to save people, the 1000 year reign is an example of how hard God works to convince people to believe in His Son, who is in the only hope man has too escape eternal damnation.
- There is no reason for the believers in heaven to want to live in the 1000 year reign on earth. They already live in heaven. It would make no sense to come to earth to live. Jesus and the 144,000 Jews will do all the witnessing to the people and be their rulers and priests also.

This is why I think the people of the 1000 year reign will need kings and priests. A king needs a kingdom. A priests needs a flock. Jesus will be the King of Kings and the Priest of Priests. Jesus can rule any from the Holy City and His appointed Kings can rule the nations of the world at that time and the priests will have their flocks to witness too. There would be no reason that 144,000 could not keep order on the planet until the 1000 years are over.

You also must consider the kinds of unbelieving people left on earth after going through the entire seven year tribulation and still did not repent. I guess this is why GOD said in the scriptures that Jesus would rule the world with fists of iron and will not tolerate any rebellion.

After the 1000 years are over, Satan will be let free from the pit to try to influence the people of the earth that his way of life is better than what God can do for him. Some will stay with the Lord, but many did not like this subdued lifestyle the Lord demands of His people. Satan and is followers will have to be destroyed because there is not anything God can do, if they still wanted Satan's way of life.

Back to vision, John saw an angel fly through heaven with the eternal gospel to preach to them on the earth. Saying (fear God) and give Him glory. For the time of judgment has come on the earth, Worship God and God only. Another angel started saying, "Babylon the Great has fallen" because she made all nations take part in her fornication. Then a third angel said; if any man worships the beast or takes his mark will receive his full portion of wrath from God. There will be no rest, day or night, for these people. They will be in constant torment. John heard a voice from heaven saying; "Blessed are the people who die from this moment on." John then saw a white cloud with an angel sitting on it and the angel had a sickle in his hands. Then another angel appeared and said with a loud voice to the other angel; "Thrust in your sickle and reap". The angel on the cloud did what he was told and reaped. Another angel came out from

God's Altar and told the angel on the cloud to thrust his sickle and reap the unbelievers and cast them into the Great Winepress of God, which is the last battle on earth. The Great Winepress was outside the Holy City and the blood run down the valley for 1600 furlongs up to the bridle of a horse.

Chapter Sixteen

John saw seven more angels having seven great plagues; these plagues were filled with the wrath of God. After seeing this event, John noticed a sea of glass with believers standing on the glass sea with harps in their hands. These are those believers who had gotten victory over the Beast, his image, his mark, and the number of his name. They were singing the "Song of Moses". Nobody but the Jewish people knew the words of the song. All that were on the sea of glass began to give God great praise, because of His greatness and His mercy and the Lord's willingness to judge mankind fairly.

After this event happened, John noticed that the 'Temple of the Tabernacle" was open and seven angels came out clothed in bright white clothing. One of the four beasts of the throne gave each angel a vial containing the wrath of God. Then the Temple was clothed in smoke from the glory of God and His great power. No one could enter the temple until all seven plagues were accomplished. John said he heard a great voice come out of the Temple telling the seven angels to go their ways and pour out the wrath of God on the earth.

These are the things that will happened during the plague/bowl event.

- There will be grievous sores those who have the mark of the beast and those who worshipped his image.
- Sea will turn into blood and every living thing in the sea dies.
- All freshwater will be turned into blood.
- Power will be given to scorch the earth with great heat
- Wrath poured on the throne of the Beast and caused great pain on all who had the mark of the beast.
- The river Euphrates will dry up to allow the 200,000,000 troops from the east to invade the Middle East and Israel at the appointed time. You can see how miserable life is going to be on earth at this time
- There will be spirits like frogs come out of the mouth of Satan, the Beasts mouth and the false prophets mouth. Their evil spirits are to get the world ready for battle in the great day of the Almighty God.

Behold, I come as a thief. Happy is he that watches for me and keeps his spiritual house in order, so he can walk without shame with the Lord. Each person must stay on guard concerning his spiritual life and walk in the world with constant hope. The Lords coming could come anytime, but I personally think He will be here at the end of the tribulation, because that is what the bible teaches. He will come to earth to end the final battle (Armageddon) before the 1000 year reign begins on earth in Israel. Which is not the final the final battle against evil. The final battle against evil will happen after Satan has been released from the bottomless pit and allowed to go out into a world that has had peace for a thousand years under the rule of Jesus. Satan will try to convince the people that they should follow him; instead of Jesus. Satan will then convince an innumerable amount of people to form a great army to fight against the saints of God. Jesus and all His saints will come on horses to fight the battle, but this battle is fought by GOD Himself, not by anyone else. God will speak and the army of Satan will be reduced to nothingness from the great fire from God. Satan is now alone and has been captured and casted into the Lake of Fire.

Then the seventh angel poured out his plague on the earth and a great voice came of the Temple of God and said, "It is done". Which means the coming plague judgments are the final judgments of wrath on the people; but the wrath on the earth is going to be greatest on the people and animals that are here. First came voices, then thunders, then lightning's, then the greatest earthquake the earth has ever experienced, then the great city divided into three parts and the cities of the world also were destroyed. There are no more islands or mountains no longer on the earth. After this event, God sent a great hailstorm of 100 pound balls of hail on the earth to torment mankind. Mankind cursed God for sending this misery on them. Even after all these things happened to them. They still refused to repent. This makes a person realize how strong (Sin) can be in the lives of mankind, were force of this degree cannot be convincing enough to repent and avoid further misery.

Chapter Seventeen

T hen John was shown what is to happen to the Great Harlot that sits on many waters (Peoples). The kings of the earth committed fornication with her; and all the people of the earth that are still alive, have been infected by their fornication. Then John was carried in the spirit into the wilderness. Where he saw a woman sitting on scarlet colored beast with names of blasphemy against God and His people on the beast. It had seven heads and ten horns. The woman was dressed in scarlet and had precious stone is and gold attached to her. She had a gold cup in her hand that contained all the filthiness of her fornication. She had a name on her forehead. This name on her forehead may help us understand the Mark of the Beast later. The Name written is: "MYSTERY, BABYLON THE GREAT MOTHER OF HARLOTS AND ABOMINATIONS OF THE EARTH". The Woman was drunk with the blood of the saints and with the martyrs of Jesus. John said that the sight of the beast was a great wonder to him.

The angel begin to tell John the mystery of the Woman and the beast shy was riding.

The Beast that John was looking at: "Was, and is not, and yet is" shall come out of the bottomless pit and be sent to perdition. Anybody that is not written in the Book of Life will wonder at this event, because the Beast was, and was not, and yet is. I think that the Beast existed (WAS) and sent to Bottomless Pit (IS NOT) and after the 1000 year reign of Christ is released by into world and (YET IS). Of course, this will the last time He will influence the people to turn against God. He and his cronies will be thrown into the Lake of Fire at God's appointed time.

The Woman who rides the beast has her throne on the Seven Hills of Rome. There are seven kings, five have fallen and one still exists (IS) and the other (IS NOT) will come later and continue for a short space of time, and the beast (that was) and (IS NOT) is the eighth king and is of the seventh king. They will go into perdition.

The ten horns on the woman are 10 kings that have no kingdom yet, but receive Power for one hour with the beast. These kings will give their power and strength to the beast. They will make war with the Lord and lose.

The angel told John the explanation concerning the ten horns on the beast. These 10 horns on the beast, these ten horns of power will hate the Great Harlot and make her naked, destroy her flesh and burn her with fire.

-Seems that Rome will be burnt with fire, because of the Great Harlot and her doings with the many peoples of the earth. For God has put in their minds to do His will and agree to give their kingdom to the beast. The Woman rules over the Great City and is the Great City, which in turn reigns over the kings of the earth.

After all these things happened; John saw another angel coming down from heaven. He had great power and glory, saying in a strong voice," Babylon the Great has fallen". It has come a habitation of all things evil: devils, foul spirits, and a cage for the hateful and the unclean birds.

All nations have drunk of the wine of wrath of her fornication and many merchants have been made rich from the abundance of her special delicacies. John heard another voice from heaven, telling the people to get out of her before the great judgment of God falls on them. Her sins reach into heaven and God remembers them all. He will reward them doubly for her works.

She has glorified herself and has lived with all the great luxuries of being great in the land. Give her sorrow, for she says, I sit as a queen and not a widow and I will not see any sorrow. Her plagues will come on her in one day; (Death, Mourning, and Famine) and she will be completely burned up with a great fire. The Lord God is the judge and executor of all unrighteousness and all evil.

The Kings of the earth who have committed fornication with her and lived with all the good things in life. The merchants, kings, or any people that partakes in her fornication will cry and scream, because The Great City was on fire and the smoke could be seen for great distances. Those far off were saying; how great the city was, but in one hour the city Babylon was burnt to the ground by the judgment of God.

This means the merchants and business men will have no business of any kind, because there will be nobody to buy their merchandise and/or goods of commerce.

Rejoice in Heaven; apostles, prophets, for God has avenged you. Then a mighty angel picked up a great stone and cast it into the sea and begin to repeat saying again "Rejoice over her destruction, you prophets and apostles for God has avenged you." There will be no more violence in the city that does not no longer exist. There will be no more music, no more craftsmen, the millstone (desire to feed yourselves) will no longer be in you, and a candle (light) shall no longer be seen anymore, no more weddings.

In Babylon the blood of apostles, prophets, and saints, were killed and has been avenged by God. After these things had happened a great voice of many people in heaven giving; honor, praise, and glory to the God of Heaven for giving true and righteous judgments. He has judged the Great Harlot and avenged the blood of his servants and the smoke of her judgment rose up forever and forever.

Chapter Eighteen

John says the four beasts and the twenty-four elders fell down and worshipped God with great praise and a voice came from the throne of God from heaven; causing all in heaven, a so great number no one could ever count. They had the voice of many waters and as the voice of mighty thundering's saying; "Alleluia; for the Lord God reigns".

The marriage of the Lamb has come and Jesus's followers has made herself ready for the Lord's Bride (Church). The Church was to be clothed in fine linen. Fine linen is the representation of the righteous of the people of God. The Lord said "Blessed are they that are called to the marriage supper of the Lamb". Then after the statement from the angel of God. I saw the heavens opened, and there was standing a white horse; He that sat on the horse was called "Faithful and true" and in righteousness He shall judge and make war. His eyes was like flames and on His head were many crowns and He had a name written that nobody knew, but Himself. He was clothed in a vesture dipped in blood and He was called the "Word of God". All the armies that were in heaven followed Him on white horses too. They were clothed in fine linen white and clean. Out of His mouth goes a sharp sword that by using it would help defeat the nations. He will rule the nations with a rod of iron and He will thread the winepress with the fierceness and wrath of the Almighty God. He had one on His vesture and on His thigh a name. He cried out to all the birds of the air, saying come together to take part in the great supper of God. All you birds can eat the flesh of mighty men, rich and poor, and the horses.

Then I saw the beast and many nations gather to make war against Jesus who was sitting on a white horse. The Beast was taken and the False Prophet (The miracle worker). He was the one who deceived the people who had the Mark of the Beast and worshipped his image. The Beast and the False Prophet were cast into the Lake of Fire still alive and the remaining forces of the Beast were slain with the sword of the Lord's mouth. The birds gorged themselves with the flesh of the defeated army.

Then I saw another angel coming down from heaven having a Key and a large chain; the Key was to open the bottomless pit and the chain was to hold the beast (Satan). The angel grabbed ahold of the Dragon and bound him a 1000 years; where he could not deceive the nations for a 1000 year period; after the 1000 years have ended he will be let loose to deceive the nations that are on the earth at this time. He will not have so much time to deceive the nations, but having little time, Satan will go all out to deceive the nations in the world.

Chapter Nineteen

hen I had a vision of thrones and people sitting on them. They had the power to judge. I also saw the souls of men who were beheaded for witnessing about Jesus and for the word of God and those who had not taken the mark of the beast; upon their foreheads and their hand. The "mark of the beast" (in) your forehead would make the mark invisible to the general public, but not invisible to God. So do not think you can hid the mark from God. It is the spiritual seal and you cannot hide it just because you cannot see it physically. Mark of beast in head could be computer chip, memory of the number of the beast and maybe a pin number of the number of the beast or maybe a tattoo of the number, if you chose the hand, it will be a tattoo or some mark

The rest of the dead did not live again until the 1000 year reign of Christ was over. This is the, "FIRST RESURRECTION" and if you take part in the First Resurrection you will not suffer the second death. All mankind dies once and then the judgment comes on all mankind. God chose 144,000 beheaded Jews to be in the FIRST resurrection, (NO ONE ELSE) after the 1000 year reign is over. The 144,000 Jews have done their duty for the Lord: They have been the only witnesses for Jesus in the Great Tribulation and also done their duty in the 1000 year reign of Jesus; serving as kings and priests during the reign of Jesus.

After the 1000 year reign ends, Satan will be released from the bottomless pit for a short time to deceive all nations into fighting against the Lord and His saints. There will be so many they cannot be counted. Satan's army of followers encircle the HOLY CITY and the saints of God and God sent fire down upon them and consumed the entire army of Satan. This is after the 1000 year reign of Christ; This is the time that Jesus and His saints will ride together into battle, but we will not have to fight; because as soon as we believers and Jesus get to the battlefield. GOD sends fire down on His enemies and consumes everything concerning GOD's enemies on the battlefield. As we saints and Jesus sit on our horses and watch our GREAT GOD destroy the last of the unbelievers.

Then I John saw a Great White Throne being set up in heaven, with God sitting on the Throne. Then John saw the dead, small and great, stand before God and the books were opened and the "Book of Life" and all were judged out of the things that were written in the books, according to their works, good or bad in their lifetime. Death and Hell were cast into the Lake of Fire; which is the Second Death. If your name was not in the Book of Life. You were cast into the Lake of Fire where all the followers of Satan would be.

Chapter Twenty

After all these things had taken place. John saw a New Heaven and a New Earth that had no seas. God was totally renovating the earth anew. John then saw the New Jerusalem coming down from Heaven and God and His Christ will rule from the Holy City.

God will wipe all tears from their eyes, there will be no more death, sorrow, or crying, or pain of any kind. Because all things have become anew and the old things have passed away. Jesus says He is the beginning and the ending of all things in Heaven and Earth. He that overcomes the world will inherent all things. I will be his God and he will be my son, but the fearful and unbelieving will be cast into the Lake of Fire. This is the Second Death.

One of the seven angels that had the seven vials of the plagues came over to John and said he wanted to show John the Bride of Christ. He carried John to a high mountain and showed The Holy City coming down from Heaven. The glory of God was visible to all and her light clear as crystal. It had a great wall, which was very high: it had twelve gates and twelve angels at the gates. Each gate had the name of one of each tribes of Israel. On the East three gates, on the North three gates, on the South three gates and the one on the West had three gates. The walls have twelve foundations. One for each apostle of Jesus. John was given a reed to measure the Holy City. The City was four square and the length is at large as the width. The City was twelve thousand furlongs (1500 miles square) and the height was equal to the length and/or width straight up like a (Cube) with the Temple in the center. Wall was 144 cubits (21inches per cubit) according to the measurement of an angel. Wall was Jasper, City was pure gold like glass. The walls of the City was garnished with all kinds of precious stones. (One different stone for each foundation) This is the list: Jasper, Chalcedony, Emerald, Sardonyx, Sardis, Chrysotile, Beryl, Topaz, Chrysoprasus, Jacinth, Sapphire, and Amethyst. The twelve gates were one very large pearl, streets were pure gold like transparent glass. God and Jesus are the temple of the Lord. There is no need for light for the glory of the Lord will be the light of the Holy City and all nations of the saved will walk in the light of the Lord. Gates stay opened all day long for there is no night time in the Holy City.

There will be nothing in the City that defiles it, only those who are written in the Lambs Book of Life. The angel showed John a pure river of water and life, it was clear as crystal that came from under the Throne of God and the Lord. On each side of the river was a tree of life; which produced 12 different types of fruit and had its yield once a month and the leaves were used for the healing of the nations.

There will be no more curse, because the Throne of God and the Lamb will be present I the city. God's people shall see His face and His name shall be in their foreheads/minds and they will reign forever.

The angel closed the chapter by saying all these things I have shown John are faithful and true and will shortly will come to pass. "God says. Behold, I come quickly and blessed is he that keeps the sayings of the prophecies of this book." John was so taken with the angel that he fell down on his knees to worship the angel; but the angel told John, he was of the same testimony of Jesus and only worship God and the Lord Jesus.

The angel told John not to seal the prophecy of the book of "Revelation" but keep it open for all too see. For the time of the end was at hand; he that is unjust let him remain unjust, he that is filthy let him remain filthy, he that is righteous let him remain righteous, he that is holy let him remain holy.

The Lord then says, He will come quickly and his rewards are with him and he will give me my rewards according to the works that I have produced. The Lord says "He is the First and the Last" and warns His people to keep His commandments; so they will have the right to eat of the Tree of Life and enter through the gates of the Holy City. There is no way to get into the City, except through the twelve gates, for outside the City there are dogs and those of an evil heart.

Jesus says the angel was sent to John to explain the End Times to the church of the Lamb of God. Jesus says, Come and let him that is thirsty for the Word of God and whoever will that wants eternal life and be able to drink the water of life freely. Jesus gives warning to all about the Book of Revelation, "DO NOT ADD TO HIS WORDS NOR TAKE AWAY FROM HIS WORD OF PROPHECY OR GOD WILL TAKE HIS PART OUT OF THE BOOK OF LIFE AND THE HOLY CITY AND THE THINGS WRITTEN IN THIS BOOK." John says, the grace of our Lord Jesus Christ be with us all I WILL TRY TO ANSWER QUESTIONS ABOUT THE BOOK OF REVELATION THAT HAVE BEEN ON MY MIND SINCE I CAME A BELIEVER IN 1971. I WILL NOT LEAVE REVELATION FOR ANY OF MY ANSWERS. REVELATION FULFILMENT IS THE END OF OUR HUMAN REALITY AND THE START OF OUR REALITY WITH GOD AND THE LORD JESUS.

(Questions) Where did the Lord Jesus say He was saving all seven churches from the hour of temptation (wrath)? Why is just the Church of Philadelphia worthy of special consideration? Why do the other six churches get different rewards? Why does each church think it will get the same rewards as the other six churches providing they do what the Lord told them to do to correct their failures and sins? There are different rewards for each church, if they correct their problems with the Lord. What happens if they do not correct the problems the Lord shown has shown them to do to be right with him? Are they still get the rewards?

- Church of Ephesus-------- he that overcomes will be able to eat from the Tree of Life.
- Church of Smyrna--------- Crown of Life.
- Church of Pergamos-------Be able to eat hidden manna, white stone with new name.

- Church of Thyatira----------power over the nations, give him the morning star.
- Church of Sardis-------------be clothed in white linen, and not blot his name out of Book of Life
- Church of Philadelphia-----keep thee from the hour of temptation/wrath, make pillar in temple of my God and write a new name on him.
- Church of Laodicea--------grant him to sit on Throne with Jesus

Things to be done by the seven churches to get things right before Lord

- Church of Ephesus-------------remember your first love, do the first works.
- Church of Smyrna--------------fear nothing, be cast into prison to be tried, have tribulation 10 days be faithful until death, need to Repent
- Church of Pergamos-----------Has not denied faith, hold doctrine of Balaam, repent, stop eating prohibited foods and committing fornication.
- Church of Thyatira--------------hold fast to what you have, keep my works.
- Church of Sardis------------------be watchful, and strengthen what remains, hold fast and repent.
- Church of Philadelphia-----------be holy, be true, he that opened and no man can shut and shuts and no man can open.
- Church of Laodicea----------------------weak spiritually, hold fast and repent, must overcome to be clothed in white, name will not be blotted

out of Book of Life, church is (LUKEWARM) there are needs in the spiritual lives for a heartbreaking round of repentance.

The big question I have with the reading of the seven churches is what happens if one or more of the churches do not repent? I have wondered about this for a long time, because there are rewards for service and punishment from Lord. An example of this: say you have seven churches and you give each one a different gift and each gift belongs to the individual church who receives it. Yet each of them believe they have a right to all of the other gifts if they do what the Lord expects of them. As I have said before, one of the churches reward is to save them from temptation/wrath and another church gets the reward of sitting on throne with Jesus. In today's world the Christian thinks everyone will receive every gift or reward equally. No one receives more than the other or less than the other. This is not biblically correct; the Holy Spirit decides what is given and who gets what and when. There is also the problem with spiritual gifts, nobody but Jesus has them all and the Holy Spirit decides who gets what, but no one gets a special gift from the Lord without receiving the power to exercise it. It does seem that there is a difference in rewards in the chapters of the seven churches, because it does imply or the churches imply that the rewards are for the whole church not to any individual church. There are many gifts that the Christian can ask the Lord to give it to him, of course, if the Church of today belongs to a universal church of true believing Christians. They would have access to all the gifts promised by the Lord to all seven churches, providing they correct the sin in their individual churches. I do not understand what would exactly happen if many of the churches fail to repent or fail to try to straighten out what the Lord said was crooked.

John was called to heaven to witness the events of the last days and write Revelation as a witness from God to tell mankind there will be a day that the sins of mankind will end and no power can stop the process. Because it is the appointed time set by God at the beginning of human creation.

SEALS:

How will the last days of human rebellion and sin be represented? How is ever thing going down? By Seals, Trumpets, Bowl Judgments from God.

1) White Horse, Bow without Arrows, Given Crown to start conquering and to conquer
2) Red Horse, Ability to take peace from earth, Kill one another, get great Sword
3) Black Horse, Balances, Food is very scarce
4) Pale Horse, Rider called death, Hell followed, Kill 25% of earth's population with sword, hunger, death, animals of the earth
5) Souls slain for testimony of Jesus and word of God under Altar, They want judgment and vengeance for their blood, white robes, wait for brothers to be killed, told to rest.

6) Great Earthquake, Sun became black, Moon looked like blood, Stars fall from heaven, Heavens rolled up like scroll, Mountains and islands moved out of place, everybody tried to hide in dens and rocks to hide from the face of God, and they wanted to die, but God will not let them die. It could not get any worse than not being able to die regardless of what you do to kill yourself.

7) Silence in heaven for a half an hour, Seven angels get Trumpets, angel at altar to offer prayers of the saints upon the golden altar, censer, fire from altar, cast to earth, there were voices, lightings, and earthquakes.

TRUMPETS:

1) Hail and fire mixed with blood, 33% of trees were burnt up and all the green grass was burn up on the earth.

2) Burning mountain cast into sea, 33% of sea became blood, 33% of the creatures of the sea died, 33% of ships were destroyed

3) Great star fell from Heaven which was burning like lamp as it fell on 33% of the rivers and fountains of fresh water, stars name was "Wormwood". Many animals and people died from bitter water.

4) 33% of sun light was reduced, 33% of moon's light was reduced, 33% of the light of the stars was reduced, a day was reduced to 66 % light and the night was reduced to 66% night, Angel flying across sky speaking with a loud voice, saying get prepared for the three remaining trumpet angels

5) star/angel fell from heaven with the key to bottomless pit and he opened the pit, the air became black from smoke. Out of the pit came locusts who had the power to sting mankind like a scorpion, they were not allowed to hurt grass, any green thing, nor any trees, They only had the power to sting those people who did not have the Seal of God in/on their foreheads. They could sting but not kill those who had the mark; this event was put on the people of the earth for five months, men want to die but cannot. The Locusts looked like little horses with all their battle gear on, they had what appeared as gold crowns on their head, they had a face of a man, their hair was long like a woman and teeth of a Lion, with breastplates of iron, They also had wings that sounded like many chariots going into battle when they took off flying, They had tails like a scorpion that sting with their tails for five months, Their King was Satan who spent 1000 years in the bottomless pit during Jesus's reign. One woe is pasted and two more coming.

6) The Angel then released the four angels that are bound in the Euphrates, they are to kill 33% of mankind, and their horses were dressed up to look like demons. They had the power to kill with smoke, fire and brimstone. Tanks have fire and smoke come out of their main gun, and the smoke like crazy from the rear when start the engines. Yet even after all this going on nobody repented for their sins.

7) When the seventh angel sounds his trumpet, the MYSTERY OF GOD should be finished as He has

declared to the prophets, little book, time is no more, John to eat the little book.

SEVEN THUNDERS???????

There is not much in revelation to understand what the seven thunders were saying. The only thing I think was going on at this time, was the angel with the little book and the little book itself. The book represents what the seven thunders was roaring about, It was main subject and the angel did say what would happen after John was told to eat the little book (it would in the mouth taste like honey, but when it got to belly it would be very sour and bitter) It was also at this time the seventh angel sounded his trumpet and proclaimed that TIME would be no more and the mystery of God will be finished. Basically the only understanding I get from the SEVEN THUNDERS; is that the effect the contents have on man. Whatever misery that comes on mankind will start off with the end of the seventh trumpet judgment and the start of the first bowl judgment. Mankind probably thinks the end of wrath is here because things are starting to calm down at the end of seventh trumpet due to the proclaiming that (time has come to an end) and (God's mystery of the ages (JESUS) have been revealed) at the seventh trumpet sounding. When the first angel of the seven bowl judgment began to pour out his bowl on earth; things start to become bitter or harder towards the end of wrath due to the difficulty on man at that time. And the hope of an end of wrath does not come. Something else to think about; the final judgment of the seven bowls (final wrath on mankind) of God's comes next.

SEVEN BOWLS OR VIALS:

1) First angel-- poured vial on earth, men received a noisome and grievous sore on those with Mark of the Beast.
2) Second angel-- pour plague into sea, became like dead man's blood, everything died.
3) Third angel-- poured on rivers and freshwater, they became blood.
4) Fourth angel—scorch men with fire, they did not repent, cursed God, because He had power to stop plague.
5) Fifth angel—Poured vial on seat of beast, kingdom cast into total darkness, they gnawed their tongues because of great pain, and they repented not, but cursed God.
6) Sixth angel—Poured vial on Euphrates river, river dried up, Prepare the way for kings of east. Three froglike spirits came out mouth of Dragon and the mouth of the Beast and the mouth of the False Prophet, Going throughout world getting people to follow them to fight God and His army by using miracles, (LORD SAYS HE WILL COME AS A THIEF IN THE NIGHT) and tells his people to be ready at all times.
7) Seventh angel-- a great voice says, (It is done) and it begins: Thunder, Lightning's, Voices, Earthquakes, Great City was divided into three parts, nation

cities fall, Babylon came to God's remembrance, and received cup of fierceness of God's wrath. No mountains or islands no longer exist. God sent 100 pound hail on the earth and the hail was most devastating on the people and animals

Chapter Twenty-one

Hhile we are in this area of revelation; we will try to figure out who is Babylon the Great in the 2015 era. In this era, many leaders of our churches believe that we are living in the last days. The woman who sat on Beast had written on her forehead. (MYSTERY, BABYLON THE GREAT, THE MOTHER OF HARLOTS ANDABOMINATIONS} is guilty of many things.

Babylon the Great could be a physical nation like the EU?

Babylon the Great could be a spiritual nation like Christianity, Islam, etc?

Babylon the Great could be a combination of the physical with the spiritual?

Is the Great City on earth today? Yes. Why? If these days are the last days before the Lord comes back and the Bible says that the Jews came back as a nation (1948) and it also says the time of the fig tree has started and this generation of Jewish generations of 40, 70, 120 year generations will not pass away until these things come to be. (40 year generation) started in (1948—1988), but nothing happened. The (70 year generation) started 1948—2018 is three years in our future; the (120 year generation) starts in (1948—2068), 2068 is 58 years in my future as of 2015. Since The Lord Himself gave generations 40, 70, 120 as a pacific time for his return.

Look at the fig tree (ISRAEL) it began to grow in May 1948 and the Jews begin to come from all the world to their own state of Israel. They have defended themselves against all foes with their own army with help from the United States. The World's greatest nation at this time was the United States and the first to recognize ISRAEL as a state. I am looking for a nation that needs to be eliminated from the world for the tribulation events to move on in their prospective points of time during the seven years of tribulation. The sad thing about this statement; there is only one Nation on earth that meets the criteria and that nation is the UNITED STATES and no other nation comes close to meeting the criteria than those nations that partake of the evil got gain of their citizens from the UNITED STATES.

I am going to give you some words from revelation that say why Babylon the Great was to be destroyed in one hour for the evil it had done to corrupt the world. I myself believe the United States will be destroyed by nuclear warfare, because there is no other way to destroy the United States, because it cannot be taken over by ground forces because nearly everyone is armed in the United States, so that's not going to work. The United States will probably be disabled from the rest of the world and not be able to inject their influence on the world anymore.

If our economy is destroyed, we will be all in the same boat, money will be of no value, and there will only be the law of survival. There will be no medical services. There will be no police to enforce any law. They will doing their best to help their own family or relatives survive, so you cannot count on others.

This is what the Book of Revelations says about "AMERICA THE GREAT" in the last and final days of mankind. It's time for man to pay the piper for all the evil he has brought on each other and refusal to listen to GOD.

BABYLON THE GREAT/AMERICA THE GREAT has been defeated and is now become the habitation of devils and the hold of every foul spirit, and a cage of every unclean and hateful bird. For all nations have drunk of the wine of her wrath of her fornication, and the kings of the earth have committed with her, and the merchants of the earth are waxed rich through the abundance of her delicacies.

For her sins have reached into heaven, and God remembers her iniquities. How much she has glorified herself and lived deliciously, so much torment and sorrow will I gave her, but she says in her heart, I SIT AS QUEEN OF THE GREAT CITY AND I AM NO WIDOW AND I WILL SEE NO SORROW. Therefore in one day: death, and mourning, famines, and be totally burned up with fire. There is no weapon on earth, except the nuclear bombs (About 15,000) on the earth in 2015. That can destroy the surface of the earth. There is a lot to say about this situation of total destruction. I will come back later in the book to answer some questions about the nuclear end of the GREAT CITY of Revelation.

The kings of the earth are standing far off so they will not be part of her torment, and the merchants of the earth shall weep and mourn over her; for there is no one to left to by her merchandise. All the fruits that your soul lusted after are departed from you, and all the things which were dainty and goodly, are departed from you, and you shall find them no more at all. The merchants of these things, which were made rich by her, shall stand far off for the fear of her torment, weeping and wailing, for in one hour she was made desolate.

Rejoice over her destruction, you in heaven, the apostles, and prophets, for GOD has avenged you. Thus with violence shall that Great City Babylon be thrown down and shall be found no more. There will be no more music, no craftsmen, and the millstone will be heard no more, there will be no more light shine in you at all, be no more weddings or brides or grooms. Your merchants were the great men of the earth; for in your sorceries were all nations deceived. In her was found the blood of Prophets, Saints, and all the people slain on the earth.

After these things. I heard a great voice of much people in heaven, saying, Alleluia, Salvation, and glory, and honor, and power unto the LORD OUR GOD: For truth and righteous are His judgments: for He has judged the GREAT HARLOT, which is (BABYLON/AMERICA) which did corrupt the earth with her fornications, and had avenged the blood of his servants by Her hand, and the smoke of her torment will rise forever. Then there was great praise by an uncountable amount of people, with the voice of many waters, and great voice of thundering, Giving great praise to the LORD GOD our omnipotent GOD that reigns forever.

Chapter Twenty-two

The marriage of the Lamb has now come and His wife has made herself ready, and to her was granted that she should be arrayed in fine linen, clean and white: for the fine linen is the righteous of saints. The angel said to me, write this down, blessed are they which are called unto the marriage supper of the Lamb. And the angel said, these are true sayings of GOD. (WORSHIP GOD: FOR THE TESTIMONY OF JESUS IS THE TRUE SPIRIT OF PROPHESY).

We have covered most of Revelation, except, the 1000 year reign of JESUS. The new TEMPLE OF GOD coming down from heaven, will it happen before the REIGN or AFTER THE REIGN of JESUS? Does the earth have to be created into a new earth, before HOLY CITY comes down from GOD? Does JESUS have sit on the throne of David made by men during the reign of Christ? What happens after the WHITE THRONE JUDGMENT SEAT is set up in heaven. There are no longer any freewill choices to be made, you have already made them for yourself, by your own will, there is nothing you can do about anything, but try to defend your actions and your sins on earth before JESUS, (GOD) the judge of all things in heaven or earth.

One of the greatest things about being a Christian, you have someone to plead your case before GOD and using His own testimony to save you and give you a future with the LORD. All sins are blotted out by His testimony, you are one of GOD'S own children.

Let's get into the 1000 year reign of Christ. Which will be a place of testing for all unbelievers, but many will become believers by the teaching of the 144,000 Jews who reign on earth as kings and priests of the LORD. Jesus will rule with the rod of iron to force the people to learn GOD'S way of life of peace, love, hope, and all the things that are good for mankind, but you still have the right to free choice to obey or not obey. (REMEMBER YOU ARE TELLING GOD YOUR CHOICE). There is a reason why those in the 1000 year reign should receive the testimony of JESUS. One thing for sure nobody can deny that JESUS does not exist anymore. Jesus is the absolute ruler of the 1000 year reign.

Those who survived the tribulation (but did not become believers in Christ) will become citizens of the 1000 year reign of Christ. There should be about 3 billion people out of 7 billion people alive on earth before the Reign of Christ begins that have survived the seven seals judgment and are going to be sent directly into the 1000 year reign. Where Satan's influence on mankind will be removed for a 1000 years. Of course, you still have to deal with the flesh side of man. Remember there is a flesh man and a spiritual man, but in the reign, there are no external forces or third parties involved. You choose for yourself what way you want to go. One way is a curse (DEATH) and other way is a blessing (LIFE).

At this time you cannot blame Satan for your sins, He is in the bottomless pit for a 1000 years. Think about it. Revelation says the Beast was, and is not, yet is. Simply saying that the beast did exist on earth, does not exist now, because he is in bottomless pit, but will exist later after he is released from the pit in a 1000 years

Most of us would think the Beast is Satan, because he came out of the bottomless pit. There are three evil powers that work against GOD on the earth: SATAN, THE BEAST, and THE FALSE PROPHET AND THEIR EVIL DEMONS. It says in revelation that the beast and the false prophet were cast into the lake of fire alive. And after the 1000 year reign has expired. Satan is being let out of the bottomless pit to tempt those who lived during the Reign of Christ. It seems to me that the Beast is not Satan, but one of Satan's top generals and not Satan, because it says in revelation that the Beast and the False Prophet were cast into the Lake of Fire still alive. Satan or Devil was sent to bottomless pit for a thousand years; this is why I do not think the Beast is Satan. How can the Beast can be Satan, because the Beast and the False Prophet were already cast into the Lake of Fire; then soon after Satan was released from the pit. I know that this has no importance to most people, but it helps clear my mind in a small way to sort out all these names of the enemies of our LORD JESUS CHRIST.

I know I am going to step on many educated toes, by discussing what and when the first and second resurrection will come to be. Let's go to the first resurrection that the book of revelation plainly and simply talks about.

I saw thrones and them that sat on them and judgment was given to them: and I saw the souls of them that were (beheaded) for the witness of JESUS and for the word of God, and not worshipped the Beast, nor His image, nor any received any mark on their head or on their hands and (THEY LIVED AND REIGNED WITH CHRIST FOR A THOUSAND YEARS, AND THE REST OF THE DEAD DID NOT LIVE AGAIN UNTIL THE THOUSAND YEARS ARE FINISHED.) This is the first and only resurrection in the last days until the seventh trumpet is sounded and the believers in Christ will meet Him in the Air and Jesus will take them to heaven; then Jesus will return on a cloud just like the angels said, when He went to heaven on a cloud after His resurrection. Jesus will come down on a cloud, step on Mountain of Olives, and cause the mountain to split in too.

The Second Resurrection will happen when all things that are to be completed, will be completed. The wrath of GOD will be finished against mankind after the White Throne Judgment. The army Satan put together after his release from the bottomless pit was so many they could not be counted. They will be destroyed by GOD Himself with a flame of fire from heaven. Satan was cast into Lake of Fire. Those people who accepted the testimony of Jesus were in heaven and those who refused the testimony of Jesus were at the White Throne judgment seat. "I saw the dead, small and great, stand before GOD; and the books were opened: and another book was opened, which was the BOOK OF LIFE; and the dead was judged out of those things which were written in the books, according to their works, And the sea gave up the dead which were in it; and DEATH and HELL delivered up the dead that were in them; and every person was judged according to their works, and death and hell was cast into the lake of fire. This is the second death and the final resurrection of man. Anyone whose name was not in the Book of Life was cast into the Lake of Fire."

I have always heard that those people who were before the White Throne Judgment Seat, were those who did not have the testimony of Jesus. Yet, why would the book of life have to be at the judgment seat if there was no one there who would or could be saved or was saved by having their name in the book of life. I personally think that everyone from the beginning of man to the end of man will be present at the GREAT WHITE THRONE JUDGMENT SEAT. Believers and unbelievers should be at the judgment. One to be saved and one to be condemned. If the Book of Life is present at final judgment seat of both the believer and unbeliever. It seems we all will be judged together and not apart.

The Book of Life seems to be the judge in final day. Everything and everybody has already been judged before they were created. The Book of Life is the record of who and how many people will become citizens of the kingdom. The believers have records of what they did in life, just like unbelievers, but their faith in the testimony of JESUS, is the only key to be a citizen of the kingdom of GOD. The unbelievers have only the records of their own lives to defend them.

GOD wanted to give His son a kingdom of his own, this is the only reason for life and what was created. He used man to create the citizens of this new kingdom. He gave everybody freewill to choose or reject the kingdom. GOD did not want anybody, but those who wanted to be in the kingdom and have JESUS as their king. There was a price to be paid, and JESUS was the only one who could pay it. JESUS had to die to give man a leader and savior from sin. We believers sin also, as well, as unbelievers, but we have faith in JESUS to clear our sin record with GOD.

Everything that had to be done has been done. It is time for the creation of a new heaven and a new earth and the City of New Jerusalem to come down from heaven. (The first heaven) and the (first earth) has passed away and the new world will have no seas or oceans. The earth has to be recreated before the New Jerusalem could be sent to the new earth. Then GOD's tabernacle will be with men, and He will dwell with them, and they shall be His people. And GOD Himself shall be with them, and be their GOD. There will be no more tears, no more death, sorrow, crying, or pain. GOD has made all things new; there is nothing left of the old earth or the things that were in it.

GOD says HE is going to make all things new, and GOD Himself told John to write; for these words are true and faithful. (He that overcomes shall inherit all things.) I will be their GOD and they will be my children.

He that is fearful or unbelieving, or abominable, or murderers, or whoremongers, or sorcerers, or idolaters, or liars, shall be cast into the Lake of Fire that burns with fire and brimstone.

John was carried to a great and high mountain to see the descending of the Holy City from GOD Having the glory of GOD about it and the light about it was as clear as crystal. It had a high wall and twelve gates, with twelve angels and the names of the twelve tribes of Israel that are the foundation of the walls. There were three gates on each side of four walls: North, South, East, and West. The city was square, and 1500 miles each way and 1500 miles high, according to the dictionary: one-eighth of mile is one furlong and 12000 furlongs is equal to 1500 miles (12,000 divided by 8) for each side and height of the HOLY CITY. The furlong measurement comes from an old dictionary that says a furlong is (one-eighth of a mile or 220 yards), or 1760 yards in a mile.

The walls were 144 cubits wide or about 252 (144 cubits x 21 inches) = (3024 inches divided by a 12 inch foot) = 252 feet wide or 84 yards wide wall. The wall was Jasper, the city pure gold, all the walls were garnished with all kinds of precious stones. The twelve foundations are: Jasper, sapphire, chalcedony, emerald, sardonyx, sardius, chrysotile, beryl, topaz, chrysoprasus, jacinth, and the 12th foundation is amethyst. The twelve gates were made of giant pearls; and the street was made of gold that looked like glass. There was no temple because GOD and Jesus were the temple of this place. The City had no need for light, for GOD and Jesus were the light and glory of the City and the saved of GOD will walk in this light and all kings will bring glory and honor to the City. The gates will always be open because there is no night. There will be no one but those who are written in the Book of Life that can enter the City.

John was shown a river of water, as pure as crystal coming out of the throne of GOD and JESUS. There were trees on each side of the river, and the tree of life which yielded fruit each month was there also. The Tree yielded twelve different types of fruit. The leaves of the Tree were used as medicine for the nations. There will be no need for the light of the candle, or of the moon, or the sun; because the glory of GOD and Jesus will be the light of the City.

There will be no more curse, and we will see GOD face to face, and His name shall be in their foreheads and GOD and Jesus will reign forever and forever. The Lord sayings are true and faithful. GOD has shown mankind the end of their existence and how their existence will end and He has shown everybody how to avoid being sent into the Lake of Fire. (THERE IS ONLY ONE WAY AND THAT IS ACCEPTING THE TESTIMONY OF JESUS.)

GOD says, Behold, I come quickly, blessed is he that keeps the sayings of this prophecy in his heart and does what the prophecy of Revelation says. Keep the sayings of this book and worship GOD.

The angel told John not to seal the sayings of this prophecies of this book: for the time is at hand for these prophecies to be fulfilled. The angel told John he that is unjust, let him be unjust still: and he that is filthy, let him be filthy still: and he that is righteous, let him be righteous still: and he that is holy: let him be holy still.

GOD says, I will come quickly and my reward is with me. I will give every man or woman according to whatever their work shall be. I am the beginning and the end of things, I am the first and the last of all things. Happy are those who do my commandments; they will have the right to enter the gates of the city and eat of the Tree of Life. "Whosoever will, let him take the water freely".

The end of Revelation says a lot about how life is going to be in heaven. JESUS talks about how things will be in the last days and what He expects of his children, and for them to understand about the new life, the old life is passing away.

GOD does say that if anybody adds to His prophecies or takes away from the prophecies of the BOOK OF REVELATION. This person will receive all the plagues of the book. If a believer takes away any of these things to change the wording of the prophecy. GOD will take his part out of the Book of Life, and the HOLY CITY and from other things, which are written in this book.

May the LORD come quickly and end the sufferings, and heartaches of HIS people, and help those who do not understand that the testimony of Jesus is the only KEY to eternal life. This mostly done at this time with the book of revelation except for a lot of interesting points I personally want to discuss later concerning the book of revelation.

I want to get into some Old Testament prophecies about the latter days that will add substance and value to the prophecies of Revelation. GOD started a long time ago to warn mankind that HE will end the evil on earth and heaven and declared a certain time it would happen, as you can see GOD uses time to push along events. Simply saying: YOU CANNOT GO FROM

A---to----C, WITHOUT GOING THROUGH B First. Actually this is the story of every human being on earth, the book I will cover first, will be (Ezekiel) is a close version of the book of Revelation; that shows the events of the end time prophecies. My main interest is to attach some verses from Ezekiel with the visions in the book of Revelation; which will help make more sense to the reader.

Chapter Twenty-three

E zekiel had a vision of a ship of some type that was not of this world; he tried to describe the vision as best as he could. Today we would call it spaceship of some kind, because we have these visions in today's world and they are common place in our world today (UFOs). Can you imagine how Ezekiel felt about seeing this vision? He described the vehicle with many details.

Anyway I am not going to go into this vision because I think this vehicle is the Throne of GOD coming down to earth and the need to say what it is other than that is foolish. JESUS did come to earth Himself to explain the will of GOD THE FATHER to the people of ISRAEL.

GOD says to EZEKIEL during this vision, be not rebellious like the rebellious house of ISRAEL: eat what I give you and when I looked a hand was extended to me with a book in it. GOD spread it out before Ezekiel, it had words within and without: and there were written: lamentations, and mourning, and woe. GOD told Ezekiel to eat the book, it will be sweet as honey in the mouth but become bitter in the stomach. Then he was told to go to the house of Israel and speak the words to them.

THIS SAME VISION WAS IN THE REVELATION WHERE JOHN HAD TO EAT A LITTLE BOOK HIMSELF. THIS TIME IT INCLUDED THE GENTILES AS WELL AS JEWS. And contained the same message in the book, but this time there were seven thunders before John was told to eat the little book; and the contents were not to be revealed concerning what the seven thunders had said. Possible that these things that are in the little book have some bearing on the seven thunders in revelation.

Another vision of Ezekiel that was in The Book of Revelation was the invasion of Israel by Russia and their allies in the last days. The word of GOD came to Ezekiel to look north to GOG and MAGOG and say, "The Lord GOD says I will put hooks in your jaw and drag you to the land of Israel with your allies and armies and weapons in the end time

Russia and its allies will descend on the land of Israel like a great cloud of people. GOG will have an evil thought to invade Israel and end the earth of the Jews once and for all. Russia/Gog thinks that those who live in cities with no walls and think they live in safety would be an easy prey to gain much wealth and substance from the invasion of Israel. The LORD says: there will be a day in the latter years that my fury will come up to my face and I will show my great wrath on the peoples who have mistreated my people in the past, present, and future. Which will also come to an end at GODs command. GOD says: I will give Gog/Russia and all that are with him plagues with blood, and I will rain upon the enemies of Israel great hailstones, fire, and brimstone from heaven.

By doing this, GOD will show all mankind that He along is the absolute ruler of earth

GOD says to EZEKIEL during this vision, be not rebellious like the rebellious house of ISRAEL: eat what I give you and when I looked a hand was extended to me with a book in it. GOD spread it out before Ezekiel, it had words within and without: and there were written: lamentations, and mourning, and woe. GOD told Ezekiel to eat the book, it will be sweet as honey in the mouth but become bitter in the stomach. Then he was told to go to the house of Israel and speak the words to them. THIS SAME VISION WAS IN THE REVELATION WHERE JOHN HAD TO EAT A LITTLE BOOK HIMSELF. THIS TIME IT INCLUDED THE GENTILES AS WELL AS JEWS. And contained the same message in the book, but this time there were seven thunders before John was told to eat the little book; and the contents were not to be revealed concerning what the seven thunders had said. Possible that these things that are in the little book have some bearing on the seven thunders in revelation.

Another vision of Ezekiel that was in The Book of Revelation was the invasion of Israel by Russia and their allies in the last days. The word of GOD came to Ezekiel to look north to GOG and MAGOG and say, "The Lord GOD says I will put hooks in your jaw and drag you to the land of Israel with your allies and armies and weapons in the end time of the latter days. Russia and its allies will descend on the land of Israel like a great cloud of people. GOG will have an evil thought to invade Israel and end the earth of the Jews once and for all. Russia/Gog thinks that those who live in cities with no walls and think they live in safety would be an easy prey to gain much wealth and substance from the invasion of Israel. The LORD says: there will be a day in the latter years that my fury will come up to my face and I will show my great wrath on the peoples who have mistreated my people in the past, present, and future. Which will also come to an end at GODs command. GOD says: I will give Gog/Russia and all that are with him plagues with blood, and I will rain upon the enemies of Israel great hailstones, fire, and brimstone from heaven. By doing this, GOD will show all mankind that He is GOD and there are no gods but Him.

GOD says: HE is going to kill 83% of the attacking army and spare 17% to go back to their lands and tell their people there, that there is the true GOD that lives with the people of Israel. GOD says: there will come a time for Israel to take things of war and make farm tools out of them. Israel will become an agrarian society and live in peace under the leadership of JESUS.

There is another great vision of Ezekiel that shows that Israel will become a nation in the end times;(the fig tree begins to grow) Israel will become a nation in one day and this happened in May 1948 and they became a sovereign state. It gave the Jewish people of Israel and around the world a place to call home.

Even through Israel is free to decide its own destiny. There forces of evil trying to destroy the nation of Israel by political, religious reasons, and by anti-Semitic reasons and the fact if anyone is a Jew; He like a disease or unwanted plague on the earth. The Jews get blamed for everything that happens in a negative way in the world. There enemies grow larger each day and the fact they are surrounded does not help their situation. (But their God Is GOD) There seems to be a curse on them in the years that God banished them to other countries, but today they seem to be a heavy stone on the nations of the world, but they have a great military to defend themselves from external forces for now, but peace will soon flee from them and the Jews will become a heavy stone or burden on the nations of the world. Then Israel will not be able to maintain peace, because the world will turn against them. There are many visions of the end times from Ezekiel. I personally think the vision of the flying vehicle as a great vision of the end times. You would think Ezekiel had vision problems, but he described the craft that flies as good as 21th century man could. How could Ezekiel describe the vehicle so accurate from his time period? It makes me feel like GOD is telling mankind that some things are what they are, in this case Ezekiel saw this vehicle as the throne of God, because it had a throne on top with a figure of a man sitting on it with a rainbow around His head. I do not think anybody but GOD and JESUS have a rainbow on their heads.

Chapter Twenty-four

I will go to the visions of (Daniel) the prophet concerning end time prophecies of the latter days. In the first year of Belshazzar, king of Babylon. Daniel had a vision of the end times at night time. He saw four winds of the earth moving together on the great sea. There were four beasts coming out of the sea. Each was different than the other. One was like a lion with eagles wings. I watched as the feathers were plucked and it was taken and made to look like a man and a man's heart was given to it. (BABYLON). The second beast looked like a bear that had raised itself on one side and it had three ribs in its mouth between the teeth, it was said to devour much flesh. (PERSIA/IRAN). The third beast looked like a leopard and it had four wings like a bird, it had four heads and the earth's power was given to it. This was the empire of Alexander the Great or the (GREEK EMPIRE). The fourth beast was the most terrifying of them all and it had great iron teeth. It would crush and brake everything in its path. It had 10 horns (ROMAN EMPIRE). As John was looking at the beast; a little horn grew out of the area were the three horns were before, and these three horns were plucked by the roots, which means that they could no longer exist. The little horn had the eyes like a man and a great mouth speaking great things. I watch these things until the thrones were cast down. The LORD GOD ALMIGHTY sit on HIS throne. HIS clothes were white as snow, HIS hair was like pure wool, and HIS throne was a fiery flame, and HIS wheels as burning fire. (This is the same vision Ezekiel saw in his vision). There were untold millions ministering to the LORD and millions and millions awaiting judgment. Out came a stream of fire before GOD and the books were opened. I looked again because of the great words the Horn was speaking. I kept looking till the Beast was slain and his body was destroyed and was given to the fire that burns forever. The rest of the beasts had their kingdom taken away. Yet they were allowed to exist a little longer (SEASON AND TIME).

In the latter days, a king will set up his kingdom and he shall be mighty in power, but it will not be his own power. The people will wonder about his ability to destroy and his goal was to destroy all the people of Israel. He will cause the crafts to prosper and he will magnify himself in his heart and by destroy many. He will even stand up to the Lord, but he will be broken by the word of God, not by war or violence. Daniel was told again to seal up the vision until its appointed time. The angel did tell Daniel that there shall 1290 days for the time of the daily sacrifice be taken away and the abomination is set up. Happy will the person that refuses to be taken away before their appointed time, which is 1335 days.

Daniel wanted to know the answer to the vision; so an angel was sent from God to give Daniel an answer. The angel told Daniel that the vision is for the last days. The end will come at the time appointed and not during his lifetime.

Daniel was grieved in the spirit about certain visions, so he asked one of the angels what the vision meant. The angel said these four beasts are four kings that rise in power on the earth, but the Saints will be in the true kingdom forever. Daniel was greatly concerned about the fourth beast; which was terrible to look upon: his teeth was made of iron, his fingernails made of brass, which could destroy and brake into pieces its enemies and grind them into powder on the ground. The ten horns on his head, three were removed, and the horn with the eyes, and the beast with the great mouth looked so much stronger than the other horns.

As John watched, the little horn made war with the Saints and prevailed against them; then the sanctuary will be cleansed.

Daniel continues his night vision as he was sleeping. Says he saw one that looked like the Son of Man coming into the clouds. HE was escorted to the throne of the LORD GOD ALMIGHTY. Where there, HE would receive all power, a kingdom of HIS own, and all the glory that the Son of GOD deserved for HIS great sacrifice for the sins of mankind. HIS kingdom will never end or be destroyed.

In the last days I will make Jerusalem and Israel a burdensome stone to the world. God will do great miracles to show the world He will take care of his people. God will get rid of all things that cause his people to offend him into taking action. All nations will go against Israel in the last days. There will be violence of all kinds against the Jewish people.

Chapter Twenty-five

ZECHARIAH: VISION IN REVELATION

It was nighttime and there came a red horse in my vision. There were red, speckled and white horses in the background. Zechariah asked the man with the horses; what does this mean? The man said, these are those who go thru and fro on the earth. God assigned them that duty. God says He is not happy with the unfairness given to the Jewish people by the Gentile world, which have lived in ease in the last 70 years. The Jewish need their temple back.

Chapter Twenty-six

I will ask some important questions and answer them if I can find a decent Biblical answer to the question.

The people in the modern world are in the last days; because Israel (The fig tree) is starting to grow from their birth as a nation in May, 1948; the Lord said that this generation would not completely die off, until the Lord Jesus comes back on a cloud to the city of Jerusalem. What generation the Lord comes back in to claim his kingdom is still open: the 40 year generation has come and gone and nothing happened. The Lord said that he would come back to earth before the generation of the fig tree (Israel) had died off; which means that if you born in May, 1948; at least one of your generation would be alive to see the coming of Jesus. In the Bible there are a 40 year generation, a 70 year generation and a 120 year generation; the 40 year has passed; the 70 year is due in 2018; and the 120 year generation is due in 2068.

So according to the Bible Jesus will be back before 2068, if this generation is the one he comes back in. We are all waiting to see what happens in 2018, the 70 year generation of the fig tree. This 70th year generation is the one that has bothered me the most, because if the Lord does not show up then; we will go into the 120th generation, which is 50 more years longer and the Lord could show up anytime from 2018-2068. The way the world is today; I do not think the world can survive that long without destroying itself. What we do to ourselves is nothing compared to what the tribulation will do to mankind.

When will Jesus come back to earth to claim His kingdom and set up the 1000 year reign? JESUS will come back to earth during the seventh trumpet blast for the second time, most likely at the end of the seven bowl judgments, which are the final judgments placed on mankind before the 1000 year reign of Jesus begins.

What is the Mark of the Beast and why does it fit into the end time prophecies? It is a mark that defines who the people have chosen to provide their needs in the final days of mankind. If you chose Satan to provide. He will see to it that you are marked to show everyone that you trust Him to provide. The mark cannot be removed. Some will receive the mark in their head (memory); some will get the mark on their forehead; (visible) some will get the mark on their right hand (visible) or in their right hand (not visible, something like a computer chip maybe). You have to have the mark to buy and sell. We will probably be a cashless society by then, and the need for distribution of goods will be essential and someone or something will have to control the available essentials of life. It is probably a fact that if a person has the Mark of the Beast and choses to supply a person without the Mark, he or she, will probably be in trouble. I will say this, no one will give you anything; they will be concerned about their own lives and the lives of their family when this part of the tribulation begins to take place. I do think GOD will think that if anyone takes something from those with the mark to survive will receive the same punishment.

PEOPLE TAKE A LOOK AROUND YOU WHEN THIS HAPPENS. LIFE AS YOU KNOW IT IS OVER; IT IS TIME TO REPENT.

What is the rapture and where is it at in the book Revelation?

The Rapture is the idea that we believers will not go thru the tribulation; but we will be removed from the earth before this happens by the Lord Jesus. Everyone that is a non-believer will stay on earth to face the tribulation, until they repent or die in their unbelief.

I do not see anything in the book of Revelation that even comes close to a rapture; except maybe, the gathering of the believers at the last or seventh trumpet sounding. Then all believers that are dead in Christ will be removed by Jesus first, then them that are alive in Jesus will be next go up to meet Jesus in the air.

The only problem with the above reasoning is the Seven Bowl Judgments come after the seven trumpet sounds and if all the believers are gone. Jesus must have took them to heaven first; then came back on a cloud and step on Mountain of Olives. They surely would not come back to earth to face the Bowl judgments. Of course, you could say that Jesus came back to take the believers away from the Bowl Judgments, but that would mean the Believers had to go thru the Seal and Trumpet judgments first before the Lord took them.

There are things that make no sense in one way but make sense in another: Why is there a resurrection before the tribulation, after the tribulation, and another after the reign? Who are the few believers that are resurrected during the reign? Remember the Reign will have the hardcore unbelievers in it. It is their last chance to repent. That is why Jesus put the 144,000 Jews in charge of witnessing to the non- believers in the reign.

(Think about this: Why would Satan be let out of the Pit to corrupt believers at the end of the reign. Would it be more likely that there are no believers in the Reign? It makes more sense that he will corrupt those who are not believers.)

What happens at the White Throne Judgment of God?
If you are not in the Book of Life you are cast into lake of fire; there is nothing else to be said or will be said in the matter. You were given time to repent and you did not repent, It was your own decision.

THEN we believers who are in the Book of Life will come to the New Earth and watch the Holy City of GOD (1500 miles square and 1500 miles high) will come down from Heaven to the New Earth by the power of GOD. The Kingdom of GOD and His son JESUS will rule their people from the Holy City of Jerusalem.

I AM GOING TO WRITE WHAT I THINK IS THE ORDER OF EVENTS FROM THE START OR THE EARLY BEGINNINGS OF THE SEAL JUDGMENTS TO THE COMING DOWN OF THE HOLY CITY TO THE NEW EARTH... REMEMBER THIS IS GOING TO BE WHAT THE BOOK OF REVELATION SAYS TO ME; YOU MAKE YOUR OWN DECISIONS. REMEMBER I REASONED IT OUT BEFORE TO FIT WHAT WAS GOING ON AT THE TIME BEFORE I CAME UP WITH MY INTERPRETATION.

Personally, I think it would fair to all concerned to realize that all of us that are alive at the appointed time of the tribulation will go thru the Tribulation. Best to accept this coming situation now and come to its terms. So you can have hope to be spared in some way; but we will face the tribulation like a believer if it be God's will. Jesus comes at the first of the seventh trumpet blast and the Bowl judgments (the last of the judgments) come at the end of the seventh trumpet blast and starts immediately.

Then after the judgments are over the 1000 year Reign will begin and the 144,000 resurrected Jews will begin their rule with Jesus and the rest of the believers will be resurrected after the 1000 years.

When will the City of God come to earth?

There are only two resurrections in Revelation: The 144,000 Jews in the First Resurrection and the Second

Resurrection at the return of Jesus at the seventh trumpet blast. Revelation has no more resurrections of any kind; according to what I read in revelation.

The City of God will come down to earth after the 1000 Reign is over; and after Satan's unbelieving army is destroyed by GOD Himself and Satan is cast into Lake of Fire forever. The only thing left to do is the White Throne Judgment of GOD and everyone will be there for that moment. While this is happening GOD will be restoring the old earth into a New Earth; because no one is on the old earth. The New Earth will have no seas or oceans and be a place where evil does not exist and the believers who live on the new earth will no longer remember evil times or its presence anymore.

I am not going to say that in the end times that there is going to be a gathering of some kind at the beginning or before the tribulation. I hope so, but I do believe that such a thing will happen. I sure do not want to go into the tribulation myself, but I do not see it happening, not if it is not written in the Book of Revelation. Why create an end time book of the last days and then wonder off on some false hope theology. I still hope it happens; but I think that if it's not in GOD's only last day's book and the reason for the creation of the book was to tell mankind; what GOD is planning to do in the order of His will. There are prophecies in Ezekiel, Daniel, and others that confirm many of the prophecies of Revelation. Take Ezekiel's vision and you have a close version of Revelation and Daniels vision is almost the same in content.

The vision of the seven churches of Jesus tells me a lot about what he expects them to do to please Him.

Many have fallen away from the faith. They had when we became believers and they watered down their faith over time. Two of the seven churches are doing well and pleasing the Lord.

Each church gets a different reward for correcting their faults and failures before the Lord; and some may find themselves in the Lake of Fire if they do not get their act together. There is one thing I do not understand is why each church gets a different reward and all the others expect to receive the same reward that the others have gotten? Let's take the church of Philadelphia; if they continue to please the Lord, they are going to be spared from the day of wrath or temptation. Many think they are going to be raptured or gathered up to the Lord before the tribulation from this verse along. Besides it does not say the other churches are going to be gathered up as well. God did not take LOT to heaven to save him; he just moved him to a safer place. As I said before, the seventh trump of God is the only possible gathering of all the believers: Dead or Alive. Except for the 144,000 Jewish believers that still have more work to do for the Lord? I imagine if there is no mass gathering to the clouds, when the Seals of God are first executed; there will be a great falling away from the faith. Remember that you could never stand against this type of wrath by your own strength anyway; you need Jesus to with stand the things you are about to face.

Earthquakes are becoming more frequent and are increasing in strength each year and there is no place in world that do not have fault lines; which are necessary to have an earthquake. A person can say, that we have had earthquakes from the beginning of time and there is no way to say, what is happening today is not commonplace in the natural order of things. Regardless of what is happening in the world of science concerning earthquakes. They are now fulfilling the prophecies of Jesus by increasing in intensity, as well as, the numbers of earthquakes are increasing throughout the world. According to the prophecies of Jesus; there are other signs of entering into the tribulation. There are people all over the world that have no food, no clean water, and there is a presence of diseases of all kinds infecting the people of the Third world; but actually the rest of the world are not exempt from disease, but it does not kill in such great volume like diseases that infect the Third World population; which kill millions in a short period of time.

The beginning of the end of mortal man and all forms of evil on planet earth will begin just before the tribulation. This will be the time that we humans will see signs of future events begin to happen throughout the world. The first thing you will notice that there many events in the Bible that are just starting to get more severe in the world; things like wars and rumors of wars are starting to be a common occurrence throughout the world. The whole world is starting to be armed to the teeth, with all kinds of super weapons. Some nations have the ability to completely destroy the face of the earth with the weapons of mass destruction (nuclear). You do not need to be a rocket scientist to realize that weapons are made to be used not just lay around collecting dust. World wars are the beginning of sorrows for mankind according to the prophecies of Jesus concerning the end time.

Another prophecy of Jesus of the coming of the end times are the great floods that that are happening now in the world. There seems to be many floods in many places and in places where they never had floods before. People are dying by the thousands from the flood water and disease that comes with flood water.

If you put these above prophecies together; you would realize that man is getting more evil each year and will continue to degrade into greater evil as time passes on. Mankind has a history of degrading themselves; it seems to be an unstoppable force that pushes man to a greater level of degrading themselves once they stop enforcing their morals and principles on themselves.

These prophecies are the beginnings of things, that will influence the start of the tribulation period on mankind; (Remember, to get to C from A, requires a person to pass thru "B" first). We people of earth at this time in history are in the "B" part of our final destination. "B" represents the sufferings, hardships, and trials we must face to get to "C" and it also represents the hopes of people to survive the "B" part of our journey. There are always travel or distance between two points of reference.

Another end time prophecy is concerned with the division of the families of man. Everybody seems to be looking out for themselves; children are turning against their parents; and the parents are starting to turn against the children. Nobody trusts other people anymore and this distrust is spreading fast throughout the world.

The Tribulation is hypnotically happening in this book to show what everyone will face soon; when the true tribulation begins. It will start at the seal judgments and go thru White Throne judgments. Remember, I am speaking for myself in the analyzing of the Book of Revelation. My interpretation of the Book of Revelation. Is my own.

John has now come to heaven in his dream and is starting to see things going on around him. He was told to write everything he sees or hears for the future and final record of mankind. Since we have covered the seven candlesticks already. I am going to start my interpretation on the Seal judgments.

Chapter Twenty-seven

SEAL JUDGMENTS:

n the First Seal judgement: John saw a white horse with a rider that had a bow and no arrows and this person was to go out in the world conquering and to conquer the people of earth, The bow with no arrows probably represents that power of the bow was available for use, but not necessary to accomplish the mission of the rider of the white horse.

In the Second Seal judgment: Red horse appears and power was given to take peace from earth and a great sword was given to kill one another (WAR). (Great Sword is probably a great weapon like nuclear bomb).

In the Third Seal judgment John sees a black horse with a pair of balances in his hand. Food is in low supply on earth and probably will need to be rationed to the poor people and were told to leave the well-to-do and rich alone for now. Apparently, at this time there were only two types of people on earth (Rich and poor) and no middle- class. You were equally poor or you were equally rich.

In the Fourth Seal judgment: John sees a Pale horse with Death as its rider and Hell following close behind. Power given to rider over 25% of earth to kill with the sword, hunger, death, and the wild beasts. This seal represents the fact that the earth is divided into different areas by the Lord and the judgments are assigned to each area. What happens in one area of earth may not mean it's worldwide. Later on in the tribulation, worldwide events will happen.

In the Fifth Seal judgment: John saw the souls of people who were killed for witnessing about Jesus and the Word of God. Those under the altar wanted revenge against those who killed them. God told them to wait a little longer, until the other believers were killed. Meantime they were given white robes to wear.

In the Sixth Seal judgment: great earthquake. Sun became darken due thick dust in the atmosphere. Moon was reddish looking. The stars begin to fall from heaven in a scattered fashion (one here, one there); there is no organization in their falling to earth. After this, the heavens begin to roll up like a scroll and that was what it looked like when it finished, it appeared to look like a scroll. Mountains and islands were also destroyed. All people (rich or poor) tried to hide from the face of God and Jesus in caves and the rocks of the mountains.

After this, John saw a great multitude of people from all nations (that came out of the great tribulation) standing before the throne of God and Jesus. They were shouting to the Lord (in white robes) that He is the only salvation man can put his hopes on. There was great praise for God and Jesus by all that were there. Even the

24 Elders fell down and worshipped God and cast their crowns before the throne of God. God tells the people He will take care of them and wipe all tears from their eyes.

TRUMPET JUDGMENTS:

First Trumpet angel blew his trumpet and the earth was bombarded with fire, blood, and hail. 33% of trees burnt up and all the grass.

Second trumpet angel blew his trumpet. Great burning mountain falls from sky and hits sea. 33% of the sea became blood or the appearance of blood. Those things that live by the sea died. 33% of sea creatures died and 33% of all ships were destroyed.

Second trumpet angel blew his trumpet. Great burning mountain falls from sky and hits sea. 33% of the sea became blood or the appearance of blood. Those things that live by the sea died. 33% of sea creatures died and 33% of all ships were destroyed.

Third trumpet angel blew his trumpet and a great star fell from heaven. It burned like a lamp that existed in those days, it probably was a missile with fire coming out of its tail. Whatever it was, it had the ability to make 33% of all freshwater bitter. The star had a name, it was called, "Wormwood". Many people would die from the bitterness of the water; which was probably caused by radiation of a nuclear bomb explosion.

Fourth trumpet angel blew his trumpet and the sun, moon, and stars reduced their light 33% and each of them had only 66% of their original light that would shine. A day was only 66% of light in a twelve hour day. Night light was only 66% of normal star light.

The wrath of God has finally came to the earth and no one can stop it. After hearing this, John says he saw four evil angels standing on the four corners of the earth. They had the power to hold the four winds to a standstill and the wind stopped blowing throughout the world and everything became real quite. About this time, a good angel came with the seal of God. He told the evil angels not to hurt the trees or grass on the earth until he has sealed the 144,000 Jewish believers with the seal of God in their foreheads. These Jewish believers have been resurrected in the First Resurrection to serve Jesus at the end of the tribulation period; and to serve as kings and priests in the 1000 year reign. The second death (Lake of fire) has no power over them.

In the Seventh Seal judgment: when the seventh seal was broken; there was a great pause of silence in heaven for about 30 minutes. Then John saw seven angels stand before God and they were given seven trumpets.

Fifth trumpet angel sounded and a star (angel or person) from heaven fell to earth and he had the key that was given to him to open the bottomless pit. When it was opened; there was dark smoke that darken the sky. After this came locusts that had the power to sting man like a normal scorpion. They were not allowed to harm the trees or grass or anything that was green. There reason for existing was to sting the people who did not have the Seal of God in their foreheads. The locusts were not allowed to kill them but torture them for five months.

Many will seek death at that time, but they are not going to be able to die.

The locusts looked like horses dressed up for battle. They had gold like crowns on their heads. They had the faces of a man and hair like a woman. Their teeth was like a lion's teeth. They also had breastplates of iron and wings that sounded like many horses running into battle. Their tails were like scorpion's tails. Their king was Apollyon the evil angel of the bottomless pit.

Sixth Trumpet angel blows his trumpet. The four horns of power that are under the Altar of God speaks to the sixth angel. Let the four angels which are bound in the Euphrates River. They were let loose to carry out their purpose, which is to kill 33% of mankind. They have an army of 200,000,000. The third part of man was killed by fire, by smoke, and by brimstone. Power is in their mouth, and in their tails were like serpents. Strange as it seems, these things John sees is like a military tank going backwards or a tank going forward with his barrel facing backwards (front smoke comes out gun barrel and when engine is running in rear of tank).

Seventh trumpet angel blows his trumpet. Great voices in heaven, saying, and the kingdoms of this world have become the kingdom of our Lord, and His Christ. Everyone in heaven gave God great praise, saying, thy wrath is come and the time of the dead, that they shall be judged. And that thou should give reward into your servants, the prophets, and the saints that fear your name, small and great, and destroy them which have destroyed the earth. The seventh trumpet when it sounds, says a lot about the Second Resurrection. Dead are to be judged and it is time to reward the saints, prophets, and your servants.

BOWL JUDGMENT:

First angel poured his vial on the earth. A very noisome and grievous sore on everybody that had the Mark of the Beast and those who worshipped his image.

The Mark of the Beast is a serious problem for mankind during the tribulation and the people better be able to recognize it and not be deceived. Remember, any mark of any kind on your right hand is an eternal NO, NO, NO; plus any mark on your forehead is an eternal NO, NO, NO. And if some chance you receive anything like a computer chip or anything in your right hand or your forehead, you cannot fool God by hiding it. So I say, it too is an eternal NO, NO, NO.

Second angel poured his vial on the earth. As he poured his vial on the sea and it became as dead man's blood (dark dull red, without life), and every living thing died in the sea.

Third angel poured his vial on the earth. All rivers, lakes, fountains of water (all freshwater) became as blood or the appearance of blood. Anyway it would not be drinkable. The angel said, to the Lord, "They have shed the blood of saints and the prophets, and you have given blood for them to drink".

The fourth angel poured his vial on the sun and it caused great heat on the earth and it caused man to be scorched by the heat. Even after all that happened to the people, they did not repent, but cursed God for sending the heat.

The fifth angel poured his vial on the seat of the beast and his kingdom became full of darkness, and they gnawed their tongues for pain. They repented not, but cursed God because of the sores and the pain.

The sixth angel poured out his vial on the river Euphrates and the rivers dried up, so the kings of the east can invade the Middle East. All 200,000,000 of them.

The seventh angel poured out his vial into the air; and there came a great voice out of the temple, saying, it is done. There were voices, thunders, lightning, and a great earthquake that was greater than any other earthquake, since man has been on earth. The great city was divided into three parts and the cities of the nation's fell. God remembered Babylon and gave to her the fierceness of His wrath. After the earthquake, there were no mountains or islands left in the world and the Lord then sent a great hail on mankind, each weighed 100 pounds. The people cursed God for sending the hail and they refused to repent to God, who had the power to stop the hail.

In reviewing the seal, trumpet and vial judgments. GOD has done everything He can do to give each person a chance to repent, with a little pressure from the judgments He sends; but they seem to make the people more arrogant and rebellious. They rather curse God, than repent, and receive the mercy of God.

There are those who have gotten the Mark of the Beast and they are going to receive punished severely for getting the mark and freely worshipping the image of the Beast. They are getting what they deserve for turning their back on the LORD and his mercy; but I have always believed that a person can repent at any time until his death. Death without repentance is exactly that, you have died without repentance and your choice is FINAL; but if you have the mark and have thought about it and chose to repent. I believe your soul is worth as much as mine to God, I would have great joy to see anybody repent even under these circumstances. As long as there life; there will be repentance. As long as a person lives there will be a time for repentance and there will be always those who chose not to repent. Regardless of what God does to them.

This is why there is a 1000 year reign of Christ; it is to show the harden sinners what life under God would be like and after the 1000 years is over. Satan will be turned loose to corrupt the world again for the last time. Most of those people will follow Satan to the final battle were GOD HIMSELF will destroy them with a blast of fire from His mouth; we believers will watch only, and not be involved in the demise of Satan and his followers. GOD has no choice, but to end sin in his creation for good. What else can He do, if they lived the 1000 years with Christ and saw what it is like to live with GOD and then think that Satan's way of life is the way they want to live? There is nothing to do but end the presence of sin and rebellion in the world. And God did end this plague on mankind and threw Satan into the Lake of Fire where he will be destroyed and no longer influence mankind to rebel against God.

The next thing I want talk about is the coming of the 1500 mile square City of GOD coming down from heaven to the new earth. I am going to say a little about the City of God; since I covered some of it before. When the LORD sends the City of God to earth. The earth will need to be enlarged in some way. I expect the earth to be too small for a 1500 mile square building; plus it is 1500 miles high. Maybe at that height, the Lord can see the whole world, from pole to pole and the people of earth can also see the City of God from any place on earth. Since God said that there will be no seas, no mountains or islands left on the earth. I can assume the Lord will just redo the earth from its original foundation and not make a bigger planet. I still like the bigger planet idea through; but God knows what He is doing and whatever happens, it is fine with me. The earth will probably be totally flat. This is the reason I thought it would made bigger is to eliminate the couverture of the planet, or in layman's terms, to always look flat wherever you are on planet. I do not know what earth would look like flat, but it would be some sight to see.

There is another thing about the City of God; that I do not understand. Is there going to be a sun or a moon, if the City is going to be lighted by the glory of God and the Lord Jesus? The kingdom will not be like anything we have seen before in our lifetime. There will be no need for sleep or food unless we just want too. The City of God is hard to describe, because God did not give much information about it.

Chapter Twenty-eight

My final conclusion of this book. I did not do much work in the political side of Revelation; such as the works of the Beast, False Prophet, and that fallen angel (SATAN) who has caused all this misery on mankind. I did cover a small part of it. It is a story for another day. I will say this to all people of the world who are trying to follow the Lord Jesus: Remember what I said about the Mark of the Beast (do not let anybody put any kind of a mark on your right hand on your forehead IN or OUT), watch out for tricks, (Do nothing that will cause your name to be blotted out of the Book of Life,) Watch out for preachers and teachers who tell you otherwise. God word is the final word about these things. Do your best to stay out of trouble until the Lord shows up at the seventh trumpet sounding. Trust the Lord to help you with the tribulation you might have to go thru, but stay faithful to the end. (What a great life we are going to have when all this is finally over)

ROBERT MARTIN SCHMIDT

Printed in the United States
By Bookmasters